The Daily Telegraph

TAX GUIDE 2004

The Daily Telegraph

TAX GUIDE 2004

PREPARED BY DAVID B. GENDERS, F.C.A.

MACMILLAN

First published as *The Daily Telegraph Guide to Income Tax 1974*

28th edition, completely revised, published 2004 by Macmillan
an imprint of Pan Macmillan Ltd
Pan Macmillan, 20 New Wharf Road, London N1 9RR
Basingstoke and Oxford
Associated companies throughout the world
www.panmacmillan.com

ISBN 1 4050 2129 2

Every effort has been made to provide an up-to-date text but
the publishers cannot accept any liability for errors, omissions
or changes in detail or for any consequences arising from
the use of information contained herein.

Please note that no reference is intended to actual individuals.

ACKNOWLEDGEMENT
The Inland Revenue forms reproduced in this book are
Crown copyright and are reproduced with the permission of
the Controller of Her Majesty's Stationery Office.

9 8 7 6 5 4 3 2 1

A CIP catalogue record for this book is available from
the British Library.

Printed and bound in Great Britain by
Mackays of Chatham, plc, Chatham, Kent

CONTENTS

About the author

David Genders has been writing *The Daily Telegraph Tax Guide* since 1982. A partner of Sayers Butterworth Chartered Accountants in London, he joined the firm in 1965 as an apprentice before qualifying as a chartered accountant in 1970. He has since specialized in taxation, focusing on personal tax. Appointed partner in 1977, and senior partner in 2000, David brings a whole career of expertise and experience to the *Tax Guide*.

Away from tax affairs, David enjoys golf, gardening and walking, and harbours an ambition to drive a steam train.

INTRODUCTION

We all want a better education for our children, an improved National Health Service, a more efficient and reliable transport system, less congestion on the roads and to feel safer and more secure in our homes and when we walk the streets. So who has to foot the bill for all these services? The Government, of course. And how does the Government raise the revenues to meet this expenditure? Mainly by taxing income, wealth, production and imports as well as collecting Social contributions from us. Any deficit from one year to the next is funded by borrowing.

The taxes covered in the *Guide* are:

- Income Tax – what we pay annually on our earnings and income from savings.

- Capital Gains Tax – paid only when we realize profits on sales of our assets.

- Inheritance Tax – chargeable on some lifetime gifts of capital and on the value of our Estates on death.

- Value Added Tax – included in the price of many goods and services we buy, mainly at the standard rate of 17.5%.

- National Insurance and Social Security – the contributions we have to pay based on our earnings or business profits and the various benefits, including the State Pension, we receive in return.

- Tax Credits – what you need to know about all the new credits.

For many people tax is both confusing and complicated. This book aims to:

- explain the basics of the taxes covered for the average taxpayer as straightforwardly as possible;

- help the reader have a better understanding of their tax affairs and, therefore, be able to take control;

- make staying within the law as easy as possible;

- offer tips for savings on tax.

This edition of the *Guide* is primarily intended to cover the Self-Assessment tax year from 6 April 2003 to 5 April 2004 and is being published at about the time you should be receiving a Tax Return for this year. I hope you benefit from the read.

1 YOU AND THE INLAND REVENUE

Ask any taxpayer the question 'Would you like to pay less tax?' and I imagine that, almost without exception, the answer would be 'Yes'.

By the time you have finished reading this book I would like to think that you will have come across at least one way of saving tax, maybe:

- another allowance or relief you can claim;
- an expense that could be included in your business accounts;
- a more tax-efficient structuring of your cash deposits and investments.

But, first of all, you should have an understanding of the workings of the various Inland Revenue departments responsible for the day-to-day running of our tax system.

The Board of the Inland Revenue has overall authority for administering the fiscal legislation enacted by Government. Although there are a large number of specialist departments within the Inland Revenue it is likely that your only contact with the Revenue will be through the staff at your tax office and the Collector of Taxes.

Tax Offices

Each tax office throughout the country is headed up by a District Inspector with a full support staff of Inspectors and Clerks. The tax affairs of employees and pensioners are looked after by the tax office that deals with the Pay-As-You-Earn affairs of their employer or pension fund. If you are self-employed you will usually find that the tax office responsible for your tax affairs is local to your business address.

Currently there are the following types of tax office:

Taxpayer Service Office (TSO)

It is your TSO which:

- sends you a Tax Return to complete each year;

- processes your Return when you send it back;

- corrects any obvious or simple errors which you have made and sends you a notice detailing the amendments;

- initially chases you up if you are late sending in your Return.

TSOs are also responsible for:

- looking after all the day-to-day tax matters of the vast majority of taxpayers whose income is taxed under Pay-As-You-Earn and do not come within the system of Self-Assessment.

- processing the business accounts of self-employed taxpayers.

As long as you comply with all your tax obligations and in a timely manner, your only involvement with the Inland Revenue will be confined to your TSO.

Tax District Office (TDO)

Often situated in the same office block as a TSO each TDO is responsible for:

- providing technical assistance to the local TSO;

- investigating the Tax Returns and business accounts of those taxpayers selected for further attention;

- beginning enforcement and recovery action of late Tax Returns or payments.

Complex Personal Returns (CPR)

The tax affairs of wealthy taxpayers with complex Tax Returns are dealt with by one of the Inland Revenue's CPR teams. Taxpayers so affected should always receive a letter telling them what is happening and advising them of the name and telephone number of their 'personal case owner'.

Tax Enquiry Centre

The address and telephone number of your nearest Tax Enquiry Centre are in your local telephone book under Inland Revenue. The functions of such offices are to:

- help with enquiries and provide assistance personally or over the telephone;

- accept payments of tax from taxpayers who prefer to pay locally;

- supply forms and leaflets.

A list of the most helpful booklets on different aspects of our tax system published by the Inland Revenue is set out in Appendix 1 at the end of the book.

The Collector of Taxes

The main tasks of the Inland Revenue Accounts Offices are to:

- bank payments of tax and National Insurance Contributions; and
- keep up-to-date accurate payments records.

If you need to telephone, write to or visit any of these offices please always give your name and reference number. You can find the address and telephone number on forms and letters that have been sent to you.

Business by telephone

If your tax affairs are handled by a Tax District which is part of a Contact Centre the following services are available to you by telephone:

- personal information such as changes of address or in your personal circumstances;
- employment details;
- claims to personal allowances;
- claims for either tax relief on flat-rate expenses (see Appendix 2 at the end of the book) or certain professional subscriptions to be included in the PAYE coding for the current year;
- employee benefits such as a company car, fuel for private motoring and medical insurance which affect your PAYE coding;
- other information such as the receipt of a State Pension;
- making certain amendments to your Self-Assessment Return;
- dealing with tax repayments due to you.

In most cases nothing more will be needed from you, although the call may lead to further action by the Inland Revenue (for example, sending out a revised PAYE Coding Notice). Where your business cannot be completely dealt with by telephone the Inland Revenue officer will arrange to send you any necessary forms or follow-up material.

When you telephone do not be put off by any steps taken to establish your identity. Any such checks are for the purpose of safeguarding the privacy of your tax affairs.

Dealing with your Tax Office

On any straightforward matter, which does not come within the 'business by telephone' services, if you want a quick answer it is better to telephone your Tax Office. You will be put through to one of the Tax Inspector's assistants who should be able to help you with an enquiry about any of the following:

- general questions about Income Tax and Capital Gains Tax;

- specific questions affecting your own tax liability;

- help with completing Tax Returns and other Inland Revenue forms;

- requests for leaflets, forms and other Inland Revenue information.

On more involved aspects of your tax affairs I recommend you put these in writing to your Tax Office. Occasionally you may want to make a visit to your Tax Office for a detailed discussion on a particular matter of your tax affairs. Where this is a long way from your home or place of work you can always visit a local Inland Revenue office or your nearest Tax Enquiry Centre.

Whenever you telephone or write always remember to quote your reference number which is:

- your employer's PAYE reference; or

- your National Insurance Number; or

- if you are self-employed or pay tax at the higher rate, your Self-Assessment Unique Taxpayer Reference (UTR). This is a 10-digit number followed by the letter K.

Enquiries

Once your Return has been processed by your Tax Office, it will undergo a comprehensive programme of checks. Any obvious errors, for example in your arithmetic, will be corrected and no further enquiries will probably be made. But enquiries will be started by your Tax Office if:

- something requires fuller explanation;
- there is a risk your Return may be incorrect;
- your Return is selected for enquiry at random.

Normally the Inland Revenue have 12 months from the filing date for your Return in which to tell you that it will be the subject of enquiries. A longer period of time is allowed where you are late sending in your Return.

> Beth Adams completes her Tax Return for the year to 5 April 2004 on 8 October of that year and immediately posts it to her Tax Office. The latest filing date for her 2003/04 Return is 31 January 2005. Therefore, her Tax Office has until 31 January 2006 in which to raise any enquiries.
>
> But Beth's husband, Simon, is slow about filling in his Return and only submits it on 10 February 2005. His Tax Office can raise enquiries at any time up to 30 April 2006.

Your Return will normally become final if your Tax Office has not raised any enquiries within the permitted time period. The Inland Revenue can only raise enquiries at a later date if they discover an error which they could not reasonably have been expected to be aware of from the information provided in, or with, your Return.

At the end of an enquiry into your Return the Inland Revenue will issue a closure notice which will include the making of any necessary adjustments to your Self-Assessment. You have 30 days in which to appeal against such amendments.

Any enquiries by your Tax Office should be conducted in accordance with the specific code of practice laid down by the Inland Revenue. If your Tax Return ever becomes the subject of an enquiry this may well be a time when you should be represented by a professional tax adviser.

Determinations

Not surprisingly the Inland Revenue has special powers to deal with tax-payers who are sent a Return but fail to complete it and submit it by the filing date. In such cases an offending taxpayer can expect the Inland Revenue to make a determination of his or her income and capital gains chargeable to tax to the best of their knowledge and belief. The actual amount of tax is based on estimates of:

- the taxpayer's allowances and reliefs;
- tax deducted at source on earnings and savings income.

Any determination can be subsequently superseded by a Self-Assessment by the taxpayer or the Inland Revenue based on information provided by the taxpayer.

Assessments and appeals

In cases of fraud or neglect your Inspector of Taxes can raise an assessment to collect tax which should have been paid on a Self-Assessment.

You do, of course, have a right of appeal against:

- an assessment raised by your Tax Inspector; or
- an amendment to your Return following an enquiry.

The procedure for resolving your appeal starts with a hearing before the General or Special Tax Commissioners. It can then move on to the courts and ultimately to the House of Lords.

Prosecutions

An important role of the Inland Revenue is to deter fraud. They will prosecute in serious cases in all areas of the tax system. Cases selected for prosecution involve a wide range of offences. However, a case is more likely to be considered for prosecution if it contains features such as:

- falsification of documents;
- lying during an investigation;

- conspiracy;

- discovery of false documents made during an earlier investigation.

The Service Commitment

The standards of customer service to which the Inland Revenue is dedicated are laid down in its Service Commitment, the text of which is as follows:

The Inland Revenue is committed to serving your needs well by

- *acting fairly and impartially*

  we

  — treat your affairs in strict confidence, within the law

  — want you to pay or receive only the right amount due

- *communicating effectively with you*

  we aim to provide

  — clear and simple forms and guidance

  — accurate and complete information in a helpful and appropriate way

- *providing good quality service*

  we aim to

  — handle your affairs promptly and accurately

  — be accessible in ways that are convenient to you

  — keep your costs to the minimum necessary

  — take reasonable steps to meet special needs

  — be courteous and professional

- *taking responsibility for our service*

  — we publish annually our customer-service aims and achievements

  — if you wish to comment, or make a complaint, we want to hear from you so we can improve our service. We advise you how to do this

- *providing a better service if you help us by*

  — keeping accurate and up-to-date records

  — letting us know if your personal/business circumstances change

  — giving us correct and complete information when we ask for it

  — paying on time what you should pay.

Complaints

Any complaint should, first of all, be made to the Tax Office with which you are dealing. Address your letter to the Officer in Charge, describe the complaint (slow service, constant mistakes) and the remedy you want (an apology, compensation).

Most complaints about the Inland Revenue's handling of people's tax affairs are satisfactorily settled by their Tax Office. Where taxpayers are not satisfied with the response from their office, they can complain to:

- senior local management;

- the Inland Revenue's Head Office;

- a Member of Parliament;

- the Parliamentary Commission for Administration.

Taxpayers who are still dissatisfied can put their case to the Inland Revenue Adjudicator, who will consider complaints about the way in which the Inland Revenue:

- has handled someone's tax affairs – for example, complaints about excessive delay, errors, discourtesy; or

- has exercised discretion.

The Adjudicator will review all the facts and try to reach a decision as soon as possible. The Inland Revenue normally accepts this decision except where there are exceptional circumstances. The Board of Inland Revenue receives an annual report from the Adjudicator which serves as a useful mechanism in identifying problem areas and required changes.

Changes in legislation

Every year in March or early April the Chancellor of the Exchequer makes his annual Budget Statement. Not only does he use this occasion to report on the nation's finances, but it is the time when he tells us about:

- tax rates and allowances for the following year;

- new or amending legislation to our tax laws.

Resulting legislative changes are published in a Finance Bill. Its various clauses are debated by Parliament and occasionally amended. Subsequently, the Bill is passed by both Houses of Parliament before receiving Royal Assent. It is then published as a Finance Act.

When the law is either unclear or ambiguous the Inland Revenue will issue a Statement of Practice indicating how they intend to interpret it. There are also times when the Inland Revenue does not seek to go by the strict letter of the law. These are gathered together and published as a list of Extra-Statutory Concessions.

2 TAX RATES, ALLOWANCES AND CREDITS

For most of us our annual tax bill is simply dependent on:

- tax bands and rates;
- the allowances and credits we can claim.

Income Tax rates

Under our tax system, the tax (or fiscal) year runs from each 6 April to the following 5 April.

The rates of tax for 2003/04 are:

Band of Taxable Income	Rate of Tax	Tax on Band	Cumulative Tax
£	%	£	£
0–1,960	10	196.00	196.00
1,961–30,500	22	6,278.80	6,474.80
over 30,500	40		

The rate of 10% is known as the starting rate. The basic rate is 22% and tax at 40% is referred to as the higher rate.

Savings income, apart from dividends, is generally taxed at:

- 20% on income above the £1,960 starting rate limit but below the basic rate limit of £30,500; and
- 40% above the basic rate limit.

Income from UK dividends as taxed at:

- 10% on dividend income within the basic rate limit of £30,500; and
- 32.5% above the basic rate limit.

Allowances

You can reduce the income on which you pay tax by claiming any of the allowances to which you are entitled.

The rates of the various tax allowances for 2003/04 are:

	£
Personal	
aged under 65	4,615
aged 65–74	6,600
aged 75 and over	6,720
Married Couples	
born before 6 April 1935 and aged less than 75	*5,565
aged 75 and over	*5,635
minimum amount	*2,150
Relief for Blind person (each)	1,510

* Indicates allowances where tax relief is restricted to 10%

Allowances on which tax relief is unrestricted are deducted from total income in working out the amount of income tax you pay each year. Tax relief for the other allowances, highlighted by an asterisk in the above table, is given as a deduction from tax payable.

Indexation

Unless Parliament decides otherwise most allowances and the tax rate bands are linked to annual inflation increases. This upward movement is in line with the increase in the Retail Prices Index during the year to the end of September prior to the tax year and applies to:

- the bands of income taxable at the starting and basic rates;
- the personal allowances;
- the married couple's allowances;
- blind person's relief;
- the income limit for age allowances.

Personal allowance

Every man, woman or child, single or married, resident in the UK can claim the personal allowance. This is set against total income on which income tax is payable such as:

- a wage, salary or business profits;

- an occupational and/or a State Pension;

- income from investments.

During 2003/04, Richard West, a married man in his early 40s, earned £25,000 from his job. His tax liability for the year is £4,249.50, worked out as follows:

	£
Salary	25,000
Less: Personal allowance	4,615
Taxable income	20,385
Income tax payable	
£1,960 @ 10%	196.00
£18,425 @ 22%	4,053.50
	4,249.50

As the table on the previous page shows, the amount of your annual personal allowance depends on your age. A pensioner, aged 65 years or over for part or all of the tax year, is eligible for the personal age allowance. There is an enhanced personal age allowance for elderly taxpayers who are over 74 years old during part or all of a tax year.

Married couple's allowance

A married couple living together can benefit from the married couple's allowance so long as one spouse was at least 65 years old on 5 April 2000.

It is the husband who should make the claim. The amount of this allowance is determined by the age of the elder spouse.

Eric Black was 78 years old in 2003/04. His younger wife, Myra, celebrated her 63rd birthday the same year. They are entitled to allowances of £12,355 and £4,615 as follows:

	Eric	Myra
	£	£
Personal age/personal	6,720	4,615
Married couple's	5,635	—
Total allowances	£12,355	£4,615

Another elderly couple, Donald and Sylvia Temple, both enjoyed their 72nd birthdays in the summer of 2003. Their total allowances for 2003/04 are £12,165 and £6,600 as follows:

	Donald	Sylvia
	£	£
Personal age	6,600	6,600
Married couple's	5,565	—
Total allowances	£12,165	£6,600

The amount of the married couple's allowance in the year of marriage depends upon the time in the year that the wedding takes place. The allowance is reduced by one-twelfth for every complete month from 6 April up to the day of the marriage.

Percy Hughes, aged 71, married his wife, Barbara, aged 67, on 15 November 2003. He receives an allowance of £2,319 for 2003/04 worked out as follows:

	£
Married couple's allowance	5,565
Less: Reduction	
7/12 x £5,565	3,246
2003/04 Allowance	£2,319

There is no reduction in the married couple's allowance for a year when:

- couples separate;

- couples divorce;

- one spouse dies.

A widow is entitled to any unused part of the married couple's allowance for the year in which she loses her husband.

A wife does not need her husband's consent to claim one half of the minimum amount of the married couple's allowance, £1,075 for 2003/04. Alternatively, a married couple can jointly elect for the wife to receive the full minimum amount of the allowance, £2,150 for 2003/04. Such an election:

- must be made using Inland Revenue Form 18;

- must normally be made before the start of the tax year for which it is to apply (except in the year of marriage when the newly-weds can submit immediately a notice dealing with the reduced married couple's allowance for that year);

- once made carries on from year to year until changed by the couple.

Without the above election the husband is entitled to the full married couple's allowance. But, if he is on a low income and cannot make full use of this allowance, he can transfer any excess allowance to his wife by completing Form 575.

Age allowances – Income Limit

The purpose of the personal age and married couples allowances is to assist those pensioners on low and modest incomes. It follows, therefore, that these allowances are restricted when total income, after permitted reliefs and deductions, exceeds a specified limit – £18,300 for 2003/04. The reduction is £1 for each £2 by which total income is more than the annual stated limit. However:

- the reduced personal allowance cannot come to less than £4,615;

- there is a minimum amount of £2,150 for the married couple's allowance.

The personal age allowance decreases first. When it comes to working out any restriction to the married couple's allowance, this calculation is based solely on the husband's income. It is unaffected by the wife's income no matter how much this is.

It follows that any benefit of the higher personal age allowance is lost when income exceeds £22,290 for a taxpayer aged 65–74 and £22,510 for a pensioner over age 74.

The upper income limits for a married man beyond which the married couple's allowance reduces to the minimum amount for 2003/04 are:

	Wife's Age	
Husband's Age	*65–74	Over 74
	£	£
Under 65	25,130	25,270
*65–74	29,120	29,260
Over 74	29,480	29,480

* Born before 6 April 1935

An elderly couple, Andrew Dawson, aged 74, and his wife Monica, aged 77, whose income amounted to £22,500 and £18,900 respectively during 2003/04 paid income tax of £3,097.50 and £2,490.40 respectively, worked out as follows:

	Andrew	Monica
	£	£
Income		
State Pensions	4,027	2,410
Pensions from former employers	15,973	15,490
Building Society Interest	2,500	1,000
	22,500	18,900
Less: Personal allowance	4,615	6,420
Taxable Income	£17,885	£12,480
Income Tax payable		
£1,960 @ 10%	196.00	196.00
£13,425/£9,520 @ 22%	2,953.50	2,094.40
£2,500/£1,000 @ 20%	500.00	200.00
	3,649.50	2,490.40
Less: Relief for married couple's allowance – £5,520 @ 10%	552.00	—
	£3,097.50	£2,490.40

Andrew does not get any benefit from the personal age allowance as his income is more than £22,290. Monica's personal age allowance of £6,720 is reduced by £300 = 0.5 x £600 (£18,900 – income limit of £18,300).

The married couple's allowance of £5,635 is initially restricted by £2,100 = 0.5 x (£22,500 – £18,300). But Andrew's loss of personal allowance of £1,985 limits the loss of relief to £115 (from £5,635 to £5,520).

Blind person's relief

This relief is given to a registered blind person. Where both husband and wife are blind each of them can claim the relief. If either spouse is on a low income and unable to use up his or her relief, any unused part can be transferred to the other spouse even if he or she is not blind.

When a taxpayer first becomes entitled to this special relief, by being registered blind, the relief will also be given for the previous tax year if, at the time, the individual had received the necessary proof of blindness needed to qualify for registration. This concession prevents individuals losing out as a result of any delays in the registration process.

Tax Credits

The new Child and Working Tax Credits have been payable from April 2003. To qualify for Tax Credits you must be:

- aged 16 or over; and
- usually living in the United Kingdom.

Married couples and couples living together as partners must submit a single joint application.

Both Tax Credits are dependent on the income of the claimant.

Child Tax Credit

Child Tax Credit (CTC) is:

- available to individuals responsible for at least one child or qualifying young person;
- paid by direct transfer to the bank account of the person (usually the mother) mainly responsible for the care of the child or children.

A child is a person under 16 years old or in the case of a 16-year-old teenager, until 1 September next after their 16th birthday. A qualifying young person is someone who is:

- no longer a child;
- under 19 years old; and
- in full time education.

CTC is made up of the following elements:

Rates for 2003/04	Annual	Weekly
	£	£
Family element	545.00	10.45
Family element, baby addition (first year only)	545.00	10.45
Child element (each child)	1,445.00	27.75
Disability element	2,155.00	41.30
Severe disability element	865.00	16.60

Working Tax Credit

The Working Tax Credit (WTC) can be claimed by individuals who are:

- employed or self-employed;

- over age 24, without children, and usually work for at least 30 hours a week;

- usually undertake paid work for at least 16 hours a week, are aged 16 and over and either responsible for at least one child or disabled.

WTC is paid to employees by their employers following instruction from the Inland Revenue. The self-employed receive their WTC direct from the Inland Revenue.

Recipients of WTC may also qualify for assistance with the costs of childcare. In such circumstances the childcare element of WTC is paid with entitlement to CTC, to the person responsible for the care of the child or children.

WTC comprises the following elements:

Rates for 2003/04	Annual	Weekly
	£	£
Basic entitlement	1,525.00	29.20
Additional couples, and lone parent, element	1,500.00	28.80
30 hour element	620.00	11.90
Disability element	2,040.00	39.15
Severe disability element	865.00	16.60
50 plus return to work payment, for 16–29 hours	1,045.00	20.00
50 plus return to work payment, for 30+ hours	1,565.00	30.00

Childcare element

— maximum eligible cost	200.00
— maximum eligible cost for one child	135.00
Percentage of eligible cost covered	**70%**

Tapering

Tax Credits taper away at a rate of 37% for each £1 of family income over a threshold of £5,060 (£13,230 where no WTC is claimed). The order of reduction is:

• Working Tax Credit;

• Childcare element;

• child elements of Child Tax Credit.

The family element and baby addition of CTC are tapered at a different rate by reference to:

• a second threshold of £50,000; and

• a different withdrawal rate of 1 in 15.

Sharon and Ken Bailey have three children, two sons aged 8 and 6 and a baby daughter born on 21 November 2003.

Ken works full time and earns a salary of £18,000. Sharon stays at home to look after the children. Before tapering their total entitlement to Tax Credits is:

	£	£
Working Tax Credit		
Basic entitlement	1,525.00	
Additional couples element	1,500.00	
30 hour element	620.00	
	———	3,645.00
Child Tax Credit		
Family element	545.00	
Baby addition	545.00	
Child element (3)	4,335.00	
	———	5,425.00

The effect of tapering is to reduce entitlement by £4,787.80 (being 37% x £18,000 – £5,060). As a result Ken receives no WTC and the CTC paid to Sharon is reduced by £1,142.80 to £4,282.20.

Alison Baldwin is a single parent. She looks after her two daughters, aged 4 and 2. She pays £250 per week for childcare costs. Alison is a successful businesswoman earning a salary of £35,000 per annum. Her Tax Credits for a full tax year work out at £3,282 as follows:

	£	£
Working Tax Credit		
Basic entitlement	1,525.00	
Lone parent element	1,500.00	
30 hour element	620.00	
Childcare element	*7,280.00	
		10,925.00
Child Tax Credit		
Child element (2)	2,890.00	
Family element	545.00	
		3,435.00
		14,360.00
Less: Taper 37% x £29,940 (£35,000 – £5,060)		11,078.00
Total Credits		£3,282.00

* £140 per week being 70% of the maximum eligible cost of £200 per week

Annual Renewal

For the first year, Tax Credits awards have been based on forms completed by reference to income in 2001/02. Individuals claiming Tax Credits will need to fill in an Annual Renewal Form for the purpose of:

- establishing that the right amount of Tax Credit was awarded for the past year; and

- providing a basis for calculating the Credit for the following year.

The first batch of renewal forms will be sent out in April 2004 for return by no later than 5 July 2004.

Changes in circumstances

Once a claimant has been granted Tax Credits, even for a nil amount, he or she has a duty to advise the Inland Revenue within 3 months of certain stipulated changes in circumstances which are:

- marriage or moving in to live with a partner;

- separation;

- discontinuing payment to a childcare provider for at least 4 weeks continuously;

- a drop of more than £10 a week in costs of childcare, again for at least 4 weeks in a row.

There may be other changes in circumstances, such as the birth of a child that should be notified to the Inland Revenue particularly to avoid losing out on an award.

Penalties and Interest

The following penalties can be charged:

Offence	*Penalty*
Failure to notify a change of circumstances within 3 months	£300
Failure to provide information or evidence required by the Inland Revenue, to include omitting to fill in and return a renewal form on time	An initial penalty of £300 followed by penalties of up to £60 per day for continuing failure
Negligent or fraudulent claims	Up to £3,000

Interest is charged by the Inland Revenue at 6.5% where Tax Credits are overpaid, wholly or partly resulting from a claimant's fraud or neglect.

3   INTEREST PAYMENTS AND OTHER OUTGOINGS

The opportunities for claiming tax relief on interest paid on borrowings are few and far between. They are for:

- the purchase, in certain circumstances, of life annuities if you are aged 65 or over;

- buying a share in:

  — an employee-controlled company;

  — a close company (i.e. controlled by five or fewer shareholders), or lending capital to it;

  — a partnership, or contributing capital to a partnership, if you are a partner;

- buying plant and machinery for use in your job or partnership so long as the plant and machinery attracts capital allowances for tax purposes (see Chapter 6).

Interest is also allowable for tax purposes on a replacement loan where the interest on existing borrowings qualifies for tax relief.

It is important to understand that the purpose for which a loan is advanced governs whether the interest on it will be eligible for tax relief. How the loan is secured is not relevant.

Apart from interest on a loan to acquire buy-to-let property, the interest on which tax relief is due is deducted from your total income in the year of payment. It cannot be spread over the period of accrual, nor can tax relief be claimed if the interest is not actually paid.

Home annuity loans

Interest on a loan taken out before 9 March 1999 to purchase an annuity (an investment providing a fixed or increasing annual sum) from an insurance company still attracts tax relief at 23% provided:

- the borrower was at least 65 years old at the time the annuity was purchased;

- not less than 90% of the loan on which the interest is payable went towards buying an annuity for life;

- security for the loan is the borrower's main residence.

The maximum loan on which tax relief is allowed is £30,000. Where a loan exceeds this limit tax relief is given on the proportion of the total interest payable equivalent to the £30,000 limit. Income tax at the special rate of 23% will be deducted at source by the insurance company in working out the regular payments to be made by the borrower.

Buy-to-let property

Interest on a loan taken out to buy, improve or alter a property which you let out is tax deductible. The interest paid each year is set against the rental income from the property and any other properties which you are renting out as part of your income from property business. If the interest paid exceeds the rent receivable in the same tax year, the excess cannot be set against your other income. The loss can only be carried forward for offset against rental income in future years.

Lionel Foster acquired a buy-to-let flat in 1998 with the assistance of a mortgage of £120,000. His rents less expenses came to £2,500 and £11,000 during 2002/03 and 2003/04 respectively.

	2002/03		2003/04
	£	£	£
Rents less expenses	2,500		11,000
Less: Loan interest paid	6,000	6,500	
Loss carried forward	£3,500	3,500	
			10,000
2003/04 Net rental income			£1,000

Business loans

Interest on any borrowings by your business can count as a deduction from your business profits for tax purposes. Provided that the borrowed money is used for business purposes it does not matter whether the interest is paid on:

- a loan taken out for some specific purpose; or

- borrowings because your bank account goes overdrawn.

Interest you pay will also qualify for tax relief where you need to borrow to:

- buy an asset, such as a car or a piece of machinery, for use in your business. The tax allowable interest will be restricted by the extent of any private usage;

- purchase a share in a partnership of which you are about to become a member, or to contribute capital for use in its business.

Perhaps, however, you have business connections with a private company? Interest paid on a loan raised so you can either buy shares in the company, or lend it money for use in its business, is tax deductible. You must either:

- own at least 5% of the company's share capital; or

- hold at least some shares in the company and spend the greater part of your time working in the business.

Employees who need to borrow to buy shares in their company, as part of an employee buy-out, are allowed tax relief on the interest paid on their borrowings.

Gift Aid

Gift Aid is an Income Tax relief for cash gifts, without limit, by individuals to charities. Under Gift Aid a charity can reclaim back from the Inland Revenue the basic-rate tax on your cash donation, thereby increasing the value of the gift to the charity. For example, a cash gift of £10 is worth £12.82 to a charity under Gift Aid.

You can:

- give any amount, large or small, regular or one-off;
- pay by cash, cheque, postal order, standing order, direct debit, or by using your credit or debit card.

For your donation to qualify under Gift Aid you must:

- pay at least as much tax in the tax year in which you make your cash gifts as the charities will reclaim on them;
- make a declaration to the charity that you want your donation to be regarded as made under Gift Aid.

If you pay tax at the top rate of 40% you can claim tax relief on the difference between the higher and basic rates of tax on all your Gift Aid payments.

Norman Walton gave donations totalling £1,560 under Gift Aid in 2003/04. Norman is a higher rate taxpayer so he can reduce his tax bill by £360 as follows:

	£
Grossed-up donations – £1,560 x $\frac{100}{78}$ =	2,000
Tax relief thereon at 40%	800
Less: Deducted when making donations	440
Reduction in Income Tax payable	£360

If you do not pay tax, Gift Aid is not for you.

Gifts of assets to charities

You can claim relief from Income Tax at your top rate of tax for the full market value of any gifts of shares, securities or land and buildings to charities at the time of the gift. The assets that qualify for this type of tax relief are:

- shares or securities listed on, or dealt in, a recognized Stock Exchange;
- units in an authorized unit trust;

- shares in an open-ended investment company;
- an interest in an offshore fund;
- land and buildings.

This Income Tax relief is in addition to exemption from Capital Gains Tax on such assets given to charities.

Jennifer Pickard pays tax at the higher rate of 40% on a substantial part of her income. She decides to give shares in a quoted company valued at £5,000 to a registered charity. The taxable capital gain on the shares would be £3,000 if she sold them. Jennifer saves tax as follows:

	£
Reduction in Income Tax (40% x £5,000)	2,000
Capital Gains Tax not payable on the gain (40% x £3,000)	1,200
Maximum tax saving	£3,200

Payroll Giving

If you are in employment there may be another way that you can make tax-efficient gifts to charity. But, first of all, you need to enquire of your employer whether it participates in such an arrangement through a Charity Arrangement approved by the Inland Revenue. If so you can ask your employer to make regular deductions from your salary which, as part of the scheme, will be passed on to the charities of your choice. You will receive full income tax relief on such donations. There is no limit to the amount you can contribute this way each year.

4 EARNINGS FROM EMPLOYMENT

Most of you will be familiar with at least some part or other of the Pay-As-You-Earn (PAYE) system. It provides a mechanism for collecting the tax due on the earnings of those people in employment. Employers must deduct Income Tax from the earnings of their employees and every month the total of these deductions has to be paid over to the Inland Revenue. The PAYE taken off an employee's earnings is treated as a credit against the overall amount of tax payable by the employee for the tax year in question. In working out the amount of tax to deduct from each employee's salary or pay packet, the employer takes into account each individual's own allowances and other reliefs. This is possible because the Inland Revenue issue employers with a code number for each employee. In turn the code number incorporates each employee's allowances and reliefs. The system allows for these to be spread evenly throughout the tax year to avoid any substantial variation in the amount of tax deducted from each salary cheque or pay packet.

The sort of earnings which count as taxable income from an employment are:

— An annual salary or wage

— Bonus

— Overtime

— Commission

— Tips or gratuities

— Holiday pay

— Sick pay

— Earnings from a part-time employment

— Directors' fees or other remuneration

— Benefits-in-kind

All directors and employees are taxed on the earnings they actually receive in a tax year.

Code numbers

I have already mentioned that each employee is issued with a code number by the tax office. In theory the code number should ensure that the correct amount of tax has been deducted from your earnings by the end of the tax year. The system can only work properly and effectively if your local tax office is kept informed of any changes in your personal circumstances that affect the amount of your allowances or reliefs. For example, most if not all notices of coding for the 2004/05 tax year commencing on 6 April 2004 were issued during the early part of the year. This is before taxpayers complete their year 2004 Tax Returns, which require a report of each person's income, capital gains, reliefs and allowances for the tax year just finished – the year to 5 April 2004. It follows that the information on which all the code numbers for 2004/05 have been based is out of date. This is why it is important you should check your code number for 2004/05 and tell your Inland Revenue office if:

• any alterations are required to your allowances or reliefs;

• you start receiving a pension;

• there is a big change in your income;

• you change your address.

You may be surprised when you come to compare your code number for 2004/05 with that for the previous year. This is because the Chancellor has already announced that the personal and age-related allowances for 2004/05 will be:

		£
Personal		4,745
Age	Personal: age 65–74	6,830
	Married couples: age 65–74	5,725
	Personal: age 75 and over	6,950
	Married couples: age 75 and over	5,795

For 2004/05 the minimum amount of the married couple's allowance will be £2,210 and the income limit for age allowances goes up to £18,900.

If there are any other changes to tax rates and allowances in the March

2004 Budget you will be sent details with any further coding notice issued to you for 2004/05.

Below is an illustration of a notice of coding forDavid Jones for 2004/05. David is a married man with two children under 16. He does not pay tax at the top rate of 40%. His personal allowance for 2004/05 is £4,745 before deductions. The first three of these deductions relate to benefits-in-kind in the form of a company car, free fuel for private motoring and private medical insurance cover provided by David's employer. Some of the types of taxable expenses and benefits are dealt with later on in this chapter. The coding notice illustrates how the tax payable on benefits-in-kind is usually collected. This is done by restricting David's allowances by the value of the benefits-in-kind which, in total, amount to £4,204.

The final deduction is for tax underpaid for 2002/03 of £110. For any one of a number of reasons the allowances given, or deductions made, in David's coding notice may subsequently turn out to be incorrect. If, as a result, there is an underpayment of tax, this is usually collected in a later year, again by restricting allowances in the coding. In our illustration a reduction in allowances for 2004/05 of £500 will result in the Inland Revenue collecting the underpayment of £110 (£500 @ 22%) from David during the year. A similar sort of adjustment to David's coding notice for 2004/05 will also be made if he sent his Tax Return for the year to 5 April 2003 back to his tax office by 30 September 2003 and asked to pay tax owing for the year (less than £2,000) through the PAYE system.

The combined effect of these adjustments is to leave David with allowances of only £41 to be set against his salary for 2004/05. His code number will be 4L. Clearly, there is a direct link between David's allowances and his code number. The suffix letter is added to the coding as a means of identifying the category into which a taxpayer falls. This is what the letters stand for:

- L   is for a code with the basic personal allowance;

- P   is for a code with the personal allowance for those aged 65–74;

- V   indicates the pensioner is entitled to both the personal and married couple's allowances for ages 65–74 and is liable to tax at the basic rate;

- Y   is the code if you are due the personal allowance for age 75 and over; and

- T   applies in most other cases, for example:

    — You ask your tax office not to use any of the letters listed above.

    — Where there are other items in the coding which need to be reviewed.

There are also a number of other codes:

- OT   no allowances have been given to you. Tax will be deducted at the starting rate, then the basic rate, and finally at the higher rate, depending on your income;

- BR   this is an instruction for your employer to deduct tax at the basic rate;

- NT   this means that no tax will be deducted;

- DO   tax will be deducted at the higher rate;

- Prefix K – a K code is given to employees whose taxable benefits exceed their personal allowances. The amount of the negative allowances is then added to the pay on which tax is to be paid. This system of K codes is designed to make taxpayers pay all the tax due on their benefits evenly throughout the tax year under the PAYE system, instead of receiving a demand at the end of the tax year for the lump sum owing.

How tax is worked out using your tax code

The coding notice issued to David Jones for 2004/05 tells him that his tax-free amount for the year is £40. He earns £21,000 per annum for his job.

The deduction for tax is worked out as follows:

	£
Pay from employment	21,000
Less: tax-free amount for year	40
Tax worked out on	£20,960

	£
Income Tax payable	
£1,960 @ 10%	196.00
£19,000 @ 22%	4,180.00
	£4,376.00

To work out the weekly amounts of pay and tax, divide the pay and tax payable for the year by 52:

Weekly pay is £21,000 ÷ 52 = £403.85

Weekly tax is £4,376.00 ÷ 52 = £84.15

To work out the equivalent monthly amount divide by 12:

Monthly pay is £21,000 ÷ 12 = £1,750.00

Monthly tax is £4,376.00 ÷ 12 = £364.67

Form P60

Shortly after the end of each tax year every employer sends to the Inland Revenue a Return summarizing the names of all employees, their earnings during the tax year and the deductions made for both Income Tax and National Insurance Contributions. By 31 May following the end of a tax year your employer must hand you a Form P60. This is a certificate of your earnings for the past tax year incorporating the Income Tax and National Insurance Contributions you paid. For most employees the Income Tax withheld under PAYE corresponds with the tax due on their earnings. Opposite is an illustration of the Form P60 sent to David Jones by his employer for 2003/04. This shows that the tax deducted from his earnings in the year amounted to £4,371.60 based on a tax code of 5L. It also tells him that he suffered National Insurance Contributions of £1,802.35 in 2003/04.

Changing your job

Whenever you change your job your employer will hand you Parts 1A, 2 and 3 of a Form P45. This form details your name and address, the name and address of your employer, your tax district and reference number, and your code number at the date of leaving. It also shows your cumulative salary and tax deductions for the tax year up to the date that you leave, and your salary and tax deductions from the last employment unless this information is the same as the cumulative figures. Your employer will send the first part of the P45 form to his tax district.

You must hand Parts 2 and 3 of the Form P45 to your new employer. He will enter your address and the date you start your new job before sending Part 3 of the form to his own tax office. The information on the form enables your new employer to make the right deductions for Income Tax and National Insurance from your new salary or wage.

You should keep Part 1A of the form for your own records. If necessary, it can then be used to assist you in the preparation of your own tax return.

Should you not have a P45 to hand to your new employer, you will find that the deductions from your salary for Income Tax are equivalent to those of a single person without any other allowances or reliefs. This is known as the 'emergency' basis. Where this happens you should either

Do not destroy P60 End of Year Certificate **2003-04**

Your employer's name and address

FIELDGATE TEXTILE CO LTD
FLOWERS LANE
FIELDGATE
TA6 2NZ

Tax Year to 5 April **2004**

Inland Revenue office name

FIELDGATE

Employer's PAYE reference **195 / F249**

Employee's details

		Sex	
National Insurance no.	FX 57 30 29 C	**M**	'M' – male, 'F' – female

Please tell your Inland Revenue office and employer if there are any changes to your personal details, for example your address

Your private address

Surname	JONES
First two forenames	DAVID
Works/ payroll no. etc	

79 ACORN STREET
FIELDGATE
TA6 2PY

National Insurance contributions in this employment

(Note: LEL = Lower Earnings Limit, ET = Earnings Threshold UEL = Upper Earnings Limit)

NIC table letter	Earnings at the LEL (where earnings are equal to or exceed the LEL) (whole £s only)	Earnings above the LEL, up to and including the ET (whole £s only)	Earnings above the ET, up to and including the UEL (whole £s only)		Employee's contributions	Scheme Contracted-out Number (For Contracted-out Money Purchase schemes OR Contracted-out Money Purchase Stakeholder Pension schemes only)
	£	£	£		£ p	
A	4008	612	16380	3899–63	1802–35	S S S S

Statutory payments in this employment

	Statutory Maternity Pay (SMP)	£ p
Statutory Paternity Pay (SPP)	Statutory Adoption Pay (SAP)	£ p

Pay and Income Tax details:

	Pay £ p	Tax deducted £ p	Enter 'R' in this box if net refund	Student Loan Deductions in this employment (whole £s only) £
In previous employment(s)				
In this employment ★	21000	4371–60		Tax Credits in this employment £ p
Total for year	21000	4371–60	*The figures aside marked ★ should be used for your Tax Return, if you get one*	

Employee's Widows & Orphans/ Life Assurance contributions in this employment ★ £ p

Week 53 payment indicator

Final tax code **5L**

To the employee: Please keep this certificate in a safe place as you will need it if you have to fill in a Tax Return or make a claim for tax credits. It also helps you check that your employer is using the correct National Insurance number and deducting the right rate of National Insurance contributions.

By law, you are required to tell us about any income that is not fully taxed, even if you are not sent a Tax Return.

INLAND REVENUE

For employer's use

Certificate by Employer/Paying Office:
This form shows your total pay for Income Tax purposes in this employment for the year. Any overtime, bonus, commission etc, Statutory Sick Pay, Statutory Maternity Pay, Statutory Paternity Pay or Statutory Adoption Pay is included.

P60 (2003-04)

BS 9/03

ask for and complete a Tax Return or send in sufficient information to your new employer's tax office so that the correct code number can be sent to your employer. If you have just left school or are taking up employment for the first time you should complete either a Form P15 or a Form P46 as a way of making sure that the right deductions for Income Tax are made from your wage or salary.

Expenses

The rules that allow you to claim tax relief on expenses relating to an employment are extremely restrictive. They seek to deny tax relief on almost all types of expenses which are not ultimately borne by the employer. This is because the employee has to show that any expenditure is incurred 'wholly, exclusively and necessarily' while performing the duties of the employment. If the employer has not been prepared to foot the bill for the expenditure involved, then the Inland Revenue are likely to take the view it was incurred more as a matter of choice than of necessity. Nevertheless, some business expenses paid personally are deductible from your income. Details of these should be entered on your Tax Return. They include:

- annual subscriptions to a professional body;

- business use of your own car and telephone;

- clothing and upkeep of tools – the Inland Revenue and the Trade Unions have agreed flat-rate allowances for the upkeep of tools and special clothing for most classes of industry. The current rates are set out in Appendix 2. As an alternative you may claim a deduction for the actual expenses on these items;

- payment by directors or employees for work-related insurance cover. Tax relief is also allowed on meeting the cost of uninsured liabilities.

Most expenses you incur in your job or employment are probably borne by your employer, who either reimburses you on an expense claim or pays for them direct. Tax-free for everyone are:

- luncheon vouchers up to 15p per day;

- free or subsidized meals in a staff canteen, provided the facilities can be used by all staff;

- sporting and recreational facilities;

- staff parties, provided the annual cost to the employer is no more than £150 per head;

- routine health checks or medical screening;

- computer equipment lent by employers provided the cash equivalent of the benefit does not come to more than £500 each year. Any excess over £500 remains taxable;

- awards for long service of at least 20 years. The cost of the articles purchased by the employer must not exceed £50 for each year of service;

- gifts not exceeding £250 in a tax year to an employee from a third party – by reason of his or her employment;

- out-placement counselling costs;

- child-care facilities at the work place or elsewhere (but not on domestic premises);

- parking facilities for cars, motorcycles or bicycles at or near your place of work;

- a works bus service;

- the cost of infrequent private transport when you have been working late and either public transport is no longer available or it would be unreasonable to expect you to use it at a late hour. Infrequent late working means a requirement to work until at least 9 p.m. not more than 60 times in a tax year;

- bicycle and cycling safety equipment made available to employees to get them between home and work;

- equipment or facilities provided to disabled people to enable them to carry out their job;

- mileage allowances where employees use their car, motorcycle or pedal cycle on business. The tax-free rates laid down by the Inland Revenue for 2003/04 are:

Cars and Vans	
— First 10,000 miles	40p per mile
— Excess	25p per mile
Motorcycles	24p per mile
Bicycles	20p per mile

Employees are taxed on payments made by their employers over and above the rates in the table. But they can claim tax back on the difference where their employers pay them less than the permitted rate.

- up to £2 per week paid to you by your employer for working at home as part of your employment contract. You are not required to produce any supporting evidence of the costs you incur;

- personal incidental expenses when you stay away from home overnight on business. The most common expenses covered are newspapers, telephone calls to home, and laundry. The tax-free limits, including VAT, are £5 per night for overnight stays anywhere within the United Kingdom and £10 per night for overnight stays elsewhere. Where an employer exceeds these limits, the whole of the payment becomes taxable – not just the excess;

- contributions by your employer to your education or training if you are an Individual Learning Account (ILA) holder. Your employer must make contributions available to all employees on similar terms.

Employee travel

Tax relief is allowed on all business travel, where journeys start from home or from an employee's permanent workplace. The cost of travelling between home and work is not allowable for tax purposes, except for disabled employees who are given financial help by their employers with home-to-work travel on public transport or by some other means.

Where the full cost of an employee's journey is not reimbursed by the employer, the employee can claim tax relief on the excess miles not paid for by the employer.

(a) Site-based workers

Site-based workers are those employees who work at a number of different places for periods of a few weeks or months at a time. Their reimbursed travelling expenses are tax free providing:

- The worker initially expects the posting not to exceed two years; and the stay must actually last for less than this time.

- There is no stipulation for an employee to return to his or her permanent workplace when each site job comes to an end.

- An employee's work on site may be considered as a single continuous period even if he or she is occasionally moved off-site.

(b) Employees with areas

The geographical area covered by employees, such as salesmen, is treated as their permanent place of work. The following special rules apply:

- All travel within the area is considered to be eligible for tax relief.

- Where an employee lives outside his or her area, travel to the start of the area is classed as home-to-work travel and is taxable if paid for by the employer.

- The whole country is likely to be the area for any employee whose duties extend to servicing customers throughout the entire UK.

The entire travelling appointments of service engineers are treated as business travel eligible for tax relief.

(c) More than one workplace

No tax relief will be due for travel from home to either place of work for those individuals with more than one permanent place of location. It is the Inland Revenue's view that a workplace is likely to be considered as permanent if:

- An employee regularly performs 40% or more of the duties of his or her employment there.

- Customers, suppliers and others would expect to be able to make contact with the employee there.

- The employee has an office, or desk and support services.

Working from home

An ever increasing number of people are now giving up on the daily commute in favour of working from home, either full-time or on a part-time basis. This is made more possible because of modern technology.

But, to get tax benefits, you must be able to demonstrate that your working from home is necessary rather than by choice. If you satisfy this test you should be able to claim tax relief on:

- A proportion of your household costs such as heating, lighting, Council Tax and telephone.

- Use of your car, computer and tools for your employer's business.

- Other expenses you incur on stationery, books and professional subscriptions for the business.

Benefits-in-kind

Employees (including full-time working directors who own 5% or under of the company's shares) earning less than £8,500 per annum including expenses are not taxed on most benefits or perks provided by their employers. In addition to those in the above list, the most valuable non-taxable benefits for this type of employee are private medical insurance and a company car.

Other directors and employees (including full-time working directors), whose total earnings, including expenses, exceed £8,500 per annum, are generally taxed on the actual value of any benefits and taxable expenses obtained from their employments. Information about your expense payments and benefits-in-kind is supplied by your employer to your tax office annually on a Form P11D. Your employer is required to give you a copy of this form by 6 July following the end of the tax year. It represents your employer's calculations of your taxable payments and cash equivalents of benefits-in-kind. It is down to you to justify those on which you should not be taxed. This should not cause you any difficulties where the expenses, such as travelling and entertaining, have genuinely arisen from the performance of the duties of your employment.

There are set rules for calculating some benefits.

(a) Company cars

The tax charge is based on a percentage of the list price of a car but graduated according to the level of the car's carbon dioxide (CO_2) emissions. The minimum charge is 15% of a car's price increasing to a maximum of 35% of list price if CO_2 emissions are above the prescribed level.

Diesel cars are subject to a 3% supplementary charge in view of their higher emissions of pollutants. This measure does not, however, take the maximum charge above 35% of a car's price.

The car benefit charges for cars with an approved CO_2 emissions figure for the 2003/04 to 2005/06 tax years are as follows:

CO_2 emissions in g/km			% of list price which is taxed	
2003/04	*2004/05*	*2005/06*	*Petrol*	*Diesel*
155	145	140	15	18
160	150	145	16	19
165	155	150	17	20
170	160	155	18	21
175	165	160	19	22
180	170	165	20	23
185	175	170	21	24
190	180	175	22	25
195	185	180	23	26
200	190	185	24	27
205	195	190	25	28
210	200	195	26	29
215	205	200	27	30
220	210	205	28	31
225	215	210	29	32
230	220	215	30	33
235	225	220	31	34
240	230	225	32	35
245	235	230	33	35
250	240	235	34	35
255	245	240	35	35

The new regime applies to all cars, not just new ones. However, special rules apply to older cars (those registered prior to 1 January 1998) which are taxed on a percentage of list price based on engine size:

Engine Size	% of List Price which is taxed
Up to 1,400	15
1,401 – 2,000	22
2,001 or more	32

Mileage between your home and place of business counts as private, not business, usage except in a car made available by an employer where:

- the employee has a travelling appointment;

- the employee travels from home to a temporary place of work and the distance travelled is less than the distance between the normal place of work and the temporary place of work;

- exceptionally, the home qualifies under tax law as a place of work and the employee travels from home to another place of work in the performance of his duties.

There are also circumstances where home-to-work travel in a car provided by an employer is regarded as private use but is ignored for tax purposes. These are where:

- a disabled person is provided with a car for home-to-work travel and there is no other private use;

- a car is provided for home-to-work travel when public transport is disrupted;

- a car is provided for late-night journeys from work to home;

If it is the policy of your employer to pay for fuel for your private motoring you have to pay income tax on an additional taxable benefit. It is the same percentage for the CO_2 emissions of your car as that used to calculate the car benefit, multiplied by £14,400.

The benefit is:

- Reduced to zero if you reimburse your employer for the full cost of fuel for all your private motoring.

- Proportionately reduced if you stop enjoying the use of free fuel for non-business motoring part-way through a tax year.

- Not charged for any period of at least 30 days during which your car cannot be used or is unavailable to you.

The private fuel benefit charges for petrol and diesel cars for the 2003/04 tax year are as follows:

CO_2 emissions in g/km	*% of list price which is taxed*		*Taxable benefit (£)*	
	Petrol	*Diesel*	*Petrol*	*Diesel*
155	15	18	2,160	2,592
160	16	19	2,304	2,736
165	17	20	2,448	2,880
170	18	21	2,592	3,024
175	19	22	2,736	3,168
180	20	23	2,880	3,312
185	21	24	3,024	3,456
190	22	25	3,168	3,600
195	23	26	3,312	3,744
200	24	27	3,456	3,888
205	25	28	3,600	4,032
210	26	29	3,744	4,176

CO_2 emissions in g/km	% of list price which is taxed		Taxable benefit (£)	
	Petrol	*Diesel*	*Petrol*	*Diesel*
215	27	30	3,888	4,320
220	28	31	4,032	4,464
225	29	32	4,176	4,608
230	30	33	4,320	4,752
235	31	34	4,464	4,896
240	32	35	4,608	5,040
245	33	35	4,752	5,040
250	34	35	4,896	5,040
255	35	35	5,040	5,040

(b) Company vans

Also taxable on a fixed amount is an employee to whom a company van is made available for private use, again including travel between home and work. For 2003/04 the taxable benefit is £500 for a van under four years old at the end of the tax year. For an older van the amount on which you pay tax is reduced to £350. Both fixed benefits also cover the cost of any fuel provided for private motoring. These rules apply to a company van with a design weight up to 3,500 kilograms. There is no taxable benefit on the incidental private use of a heavy commercial vehicle with a design weight exceeding 3,500 kilograms.

(c) Pooled vehicles

The private use of a car or van from an employer's pool of vehicles will not give rise to a tax charge on an employee provided:

- Any home-to-work travel is merely incidental to business use.

- The vehicle is not garaged at or near the employee's home overnight.

(d) Living accommodation

In some trades it is established practice for the employer to provide living accommodation. This can also be desirable where there is a security risk. No Income Tax liability arises in either sort of situation.

In other circumstances Income Tax is chargeable on the annual value of the property after deducting any rent paid for it. The annual value of property for these purposes is broadly equivalent to the gross rateable value. Estimated rateable values will be used for new properties which do not appear on the domestic rating lists. An additional tax charge must be faced where the accommodation costs more than £75,000. This is worked out by applying the Inland Revenue's official interest rate (see below) at the beginning of the tax year to the excess of the cost price over £75,000.

(e) Beneficial loans

Loans from an employer that are either interest free or where the interest charged by the employer is below a commercial rate can give rise to a taxable benefit. The benefit is calculated by applying the Inland Revenue's official rate of interest to the loan. For the 2003/04 tax year the rate is 5%. The benefit is reduced by any interest actually paid on the loan. No charge to tax arises where all an employee's cheap or interest-free loans, excluding loans that qualify for tax relief, total no more than £5,000. A tax charge is also avoided where the loan is for a purpose on which the interest would qualify for tax relief (see Chapter 3).

(f) Medical insurance

You will be taxed on private medical insurance premiums paid by your employer for you or other members of your family. If you go abroad on business then the cost of medical insurance cover, or actual medical treatment overseas, is not taxable on you as a benefit.

(g) Relocation expenses

An employee who changes his job, or is relocated by his employer, is not taxed on the costs of a relocation package up to £8,000. This limit applies to each job-related move. There are specific definitions for the removal expenses and benefits that qualify for exemption within the monetary limit.

Employee share ownership

There are a variety of share, profit sharing and share option schemes, all offering different investment limits and tax reliefs – some more generous than others.

(a) Under an All-Employee Share Scheme:

- employers can give employees up to £3,000 of shares free of tax and National Insurance;
- some or all of these shares can be awarded to employees for reaching performance targets;

- employees are able to buy partnership shares out of their pre-tax salary or wage up to a maximum of 10% of salary or £1,500 a year, free of tax and National Insurance;

- employers can match partnership shares by giving employees up to 2 free shares for each partnership share they buy;

- employees who sell their shares are liable to Capital Gains Tax only on any increase in the value of their shares after they come out of a plan;

- free and matching shares must normally be kept in the plan for at least 3 years – employees can take partnership shares out of the plan at any time;

- shares must come out of the plan when employees leave and some employees may lose their free and matching shares if they leave their jobs within 3 years of getting the shares;

- dividends, up to £1,500 annually, paid on the shares are tax free providing they are reinvested in additional shares in the company and retained for at least 3 years;

- employees who keep their shares in a plan for 5 years pay no Income Tax or National Insurance on those shares;

- employees who take their shares out of a plan after 3 years pay Income Tax and National Insurance on no more than the initial value of the shares – any increase in the value of their shares while in the plan is free of Income Tax and National Insurance;

- Capital Gains Tax roll-over relief is available for existing shareholders of smaller companies who want to sell their shares to a new plan trust to be used for the benefit of employees.

(b) The main features of a Savings-Related Share Option Scheme are:

- it operates in combination with either a bank or building society SAYE savings contract under which employees save a fixed regular amount each month;

- the maximum amount that can be saved is £250 per month over either a 3- or 5-year period;

- the price at which options can be offered to directors and employees cannot be less than 80% of the market value of the shares at the time the options are granted;

- the receipt of the options and any increase in the value of the shares between the time that the options are granted and the date when they are exercised are free of Income Tax.

(c) Under an Approved Profit-Sharing Scheme:

- a company makes an allocation of profits to Trustees who, in turn, use the contribution in acquiring shares in the company which are subsequently allotted to employees;

- the limit on the market value of shares which may be appropriated to any one individual in each tax year is 10% of salary with a minimum limit of £3,000 and a maximum of £8,000;

- there is no Income Tax liability when the shares are set aside nor if they are retained by the Trustees of the scheme for 3 years.

(d) Inland Revenue Approved Share Option Plan:

- no liability to Income Tax is imposed on a director or employee who acquires, or disposes of, ordinary shares under such a plan;

- the market value of shares, at the time of the grant of the option, over which an individual holds unexercised rights under the plan must not exceed £30,000;

- an option must be exercised not less than 3, or more than 10, years after it is granted, nor under 3 years after a previous exercise;

- the gain is measured by the difference between the sale proceeds and the cost of acquiring the shares, and is charged to Capital Gains Tax at the time of disposal;

- the price payable must be fixed at the time of the grant and must not be less than the market value of the shares at that date;

- options granted before 17 July 1995 under then approved schemes continue to qualify for tax relief on exercise even if they exceed the £30,000 ceiling now applying to company share option plans.

Enterprise Management Incentives

Enterprise Management Incentives have been designed to help small companies attract and retain the key people they need and to reward employees for taking a risk by investing their time and skills in helping small companies achieve their potential.

Companies can grant share options to employees worth up to £100,000 at the time of grant, normally without any charge to Income Tax or National Insurance. Moreover, when the shares are sold, Capital Gains Tax taper relief normally starts from the date when the options were granted.

A qualifying employee is one who must spend at least 25 hours a week or, if less, 75% of their working time, on the business of that company.

Payments on termination of employment

It is common practice for an employee to be paid a lump sum on the termination of an employment. If the right to receive the payment arose during the period of employment then it is taxable in full in the same way as other earnings. Otherwise the lump sum payment is either wholly or partly tax free. The occasions when the payments are free of tax are:

- where the employment ceases because of the accidental death, injury or disability of the employee;

- where most of the employee's time was spent working overseas for the employer;

- where the lump sum payment is made at a time other than on death or retirement. The first £30,000 is then tax free. Only the excess of any payment over £30,000 is taxable.

Any statutory redundancy payment you receive, although exempt from tax itself, has to be counted in with any other lump sum payment from your employer in working out the tax due on the lump sum.

Redundancy and employment termination settlements often provide for some benefits, such as membership of a company medical insurance scheme, to continue after termination. Such payments and benefits are taxed only to the extent they arise, and in the year in which they are received or enjoyed.

Patrick Bond lost his job in July 2003. Under his employment termination settlement he received lump sum redundancy payments of £25,000 and £15,000 on 23 July 2003 and 16 April 2004 respectively. He was also allowed to remain a member of his employer's company medical insurance scheme for three years at an annual cost of £800.

Patrick's total redundancy package for 2003/04 comes to £25,800. As this is below the £30,000 exemption limit he does not pay tax on that part of the package he received and enjoyed in 2003/04. The £4,200 balance of the exemption limit is carried forward to 2004/05 to be set against the cash payment of £15,000 and the medical insurance benefit of £800. In 2004/05, therefore, Patrick's employer will deduct tax at the basic rate on £11,600.

5 VALUE ADDED TAX

Although Value Added Tax (VAT) applies throughout Europe, more and more countries outside the European Union are now adopting it as a system for taxing what people spend. After setting the level for the standard rate, governments are able to decide what areas of expenditure should qualify for relief, and how relief should be given. The tax can then be collected quite cheaply.

Customs and Excise administer VAT. A wide range of publications is available on their website – www.hmce.gov.uk – and hard copies of material can be downloaded or obtained from the National Advice Service (NAS). The NAS is the main contact point for businesses nowadays. The telephone number is 0845 010 9000 and all calls are logged. Callers are asked to give their postcode or VAT registration number (if they have one) and, if you do call, a note of the allocated reference should be made just in case you ever need to refer back to it later on. If an enquiry happens to be of a technical nature, I suggest the details are set out fully in a letter to the VAT Business Advice Centre covering the area where your business is based. You can find the address of the one nearest to you in the telephone directory.

VAT is a self-assessed tax on supplies made by businesses. The following paragraphs give those who are new to the tax, or who have little experience of it, an insight into some of the rules and more common problems. Also mentioned are the procedures Customs have introduced to help smaller businesses.

Rates of VAT

The majority of goods and services supplied in the UK are liable to tax at the standard rate of 17.5%. Among the broad areas where relief has been granted are:

- Zero rated supplies

    — Food sold in shops

    — Books and newspapers

— Construction of new houses

— Passenger transport

— Exports of goods

- Supplies liable at 5%

    — Domestic fuel and power

    — Renovations and alterations of dwellings

    — Residential conversions

- Exempt supplies

    — Education

    — Health and welfare

    — Insurance

    — Land

    — Finance and banking transactions

It is important to realize that zero, 5% and 17.5% are all rates of tax, since the time for deciding whether, and, if so, when, to apply for registration depends upon the level of taxable supplies made. The income from any exempt supplies does not count towards the registration limit.

Registration

If your business is just starting, it is unlikely you will have to register immediately: only when the value of your taxable supplies reaches £56,000 in a 'rolling' period of 12 months is application compulsory.

It is vital that you do not delay submitting an application for registration as soon as it has to be made. Form VAT 1 has to be used for this purpose. This has to be completed no later than 30 days from the end of the month after the one in which your turnover exceeds the £56,000 limit. Registration would then be effective from the beginning of the next month.

Simon Potter commenced in business on 1 May 2003. Turnover in what would be taxable supplies reflected a steady increase to start with but then went up quite sharply towards the end of his first year as the following table shows:

		Turnover £			
2003	May	1,000			
	June	2,000			
	July	2,000			
	August	3,000			
	September	4,000	45,000	57,000	77,000
	October	4,000			
	November	5,000			
	December	6,000			
2004	January	8,000			
	February	10,000			
	March	12,000			
	April	20,000			

As turnover in the period from 1 May 2003 to 28 February 2004 was less than £56,000 there was no requirement to register. Turnover did exceed the threshold at the end of March 2004 and registration had, therefore, to be applied for during April 2004. However, since the date from which registration would take effect would be 1 May 2004, tax would not have to be charged until then. This would mean that not only the supplies throughout the earlier part of the trading period but also during April, when in that month alone they totalled £20,000, would not have to bear tax.

There is no escape from registration unless Customs can be convinced that either

- there was expected to be a drop in taxable turnover so that, from then on, it would remain at an annual level of less than £54,000, or

- the business would be one where, if registration was in place, repayments of VAT would normally have to be made.

Requests not to be registered would, in these circumstances, normally be granted, provided that your VAT Business Advice Centre was told afterwards of any changes which might alter the position.

Do not delay registering if you happen to buy an existing business, such as a shop, where the previous owner was already registered. The turnover build-up to £56,000 from the time you take on the business does not then apply: the turnover before you bought the business is taken into account as well. Sometimes it is possible for the registration number of the previous owner to be transferred to you.

Sometimes there are benefits in registering even though turnover does not come up to the compulsory registration limit. Voluntary registrations of this nature are allowed if you can show that you are, or will be, making some taxable supplies. In this way VAT incurred on your business expenses may be claimed back, including the VAT paid on assets like computers and printers on hand at the time of registration, as well as on certain business start-up costs.

Shortly after you have completed and submitted the registration forms, you should receive a letter advising you of your registration number. Your formal certificate will follow a week or two later. One or two notices or leaflets of a general nature may be sent to you with this correspondence. There may be more information that would be of interest to you and your business. Appendix 3 at the end of the book lists some of the VAT notices currently available. Always remember that the NAS is there to help you and will, upon request, forward whatever you think that you need if you do not have the facility to access and obtain material from the Customs website.

Penalties for late registration

New businesses that do not keep an eye on how their turnover is progressing can be caught out by a scaled penalty imposed for not registering when they should. The penalty is calculated as follows:

Registration not more than 9 months late	5%
Registration over 9 months but not more than 18 months late	10%
Registration more than 18 months late	15%

The penalty is based on the net tax due for the period from the time registration should have started to the date the VAT 1 Form is received by Customs or liability to be registered is discovered. There is a minimum penalty of £50. The back-tax must also be paid although it may be possible to do so in stages. Lateness in registering can also result in failure to qualify for certain benefits available to a newly registered business.

Help from Customs

It is the policy of Customs to try to make contact with new businesses soon after they have become registered so that:

- Any queries which may already have arisen can then be resolved.

- You can be offered videos on various aspects of the tax, an opportunity to attend a seminar or, alternatively, a one-to-one meeting to discuss matters of a more individual nature.

- The advantages of the simplification measures available to the smaller businesses can be pointed out to you.

Every opportunity to learn more about the tax should be taken since this book only has space to touch on certain areas of more general interest and importance.

It is unusual these days for a hard-line approach to be adopted by Customs when smaller businesses, new to VAT, run into difficulties with preparing their first one or two VAT Returns or paying the tax shown to be due. Any initial hiccups are, however, expected to be only short term: when businesses have been up and running for a while, they are expected to be better able to cope with VAT for themselves – especially with the NAS to fall back on for general guidance and help.

Records and accounting

Output tax is what you are liable for on the supplies you make (outputs) and input tax is on the purchases you receive (inputs). Whether or not you decide to use schemes available for simplifying your VAT accounting, you should keep a copy of every invoice issued for supplies made by your business. It is recommended that an analysed listing should be made of them which at least includes the following:

Invoice		Customer	VAT excl Value	VAT	Gross Value	Date payment received
No	Date					
			£	£	£	

Similarly, and unless you have been allowed to use the Flat Rate Scheme, purchase invoices should be analysed in your records and filed by you in such a way that it is possible to trace any item where input tax is claimed to the tax invoice for the purchase.

Totalling your outputs and inputs monthly should make it fairly straight-forward to bring together the details for the VAT accounting periods shown on your certificate of registration. A summary of the monthly tax totals can be noted in a VAT Account which acts as a link between your own records and the VAT Return – Form VAT 100 – which will be sent to you. If you are allocated quarters in line with the calendar quarters and you account for VAT on the basis of invoices raised and received, the VAT Account may, for the January to March period, be like this:

VAT Account Period 1 January 2004 to 31 March 2004

	£	£
Output Tax		
January	2,470	
February	2,360	
March	2,520	
Total	£7,350	7,350
Input Tax		
January	910	
February	820	
March	680	
Total	£2,410	2,410
Net amount due		£4,940

The figures in your VAT Account and the tax-exclusive values of your out-puts and inputs will put you in a position to complete the various boxes on your VAT Return.

When the Return ends up showing an amount of tax payable to the Customs and Excise you should send it off and pay what is due. If the

VAT claimable on the purchases for the business exceeds the VAT on the supplies you have made to customers or clients, the Return will show you are entitled to a repayment. It is likely this will be sent direct to your bank account although it may be subject to verification before you receive the refund.

You can request that your quarterly VAT Return periods are set to tie in with your financial year if you wish.

Input tax

The actual amount of input tax on purchases does not matter quite so much when the Flat Rate Scheme is used. For other businesses it is only the input tax on the costs of the business which can be claimed when VAT returns are completed. Sometimes expenses may be incurred where the input tax cannot be claimed at all. Examples are business entertaining and private purchases paid for by your business. Occasionally there may be a need to apportion input tax such as that on home telephone bills, which are partly for business and partly for private purposes. Apportionment is best done on a percentage basis which, provided that it is reasonable, Customs can be expected to go along with.

Motor cars and fuel

Businesses that are directly concerned with motoring, like new car dealers, vehicle hirers, taxi drivers or driving schools, may be able to claim back in full the input tax on cars which they buy or lease. The input tax cannot be claimed on cars bought by other businesses and made available for private use. With car leases, however, it may be possible to claim 50% of the input tax on the rental payments.

As for motor fuel, most businesses choose between two basic ways for dealing with input tax. All input tax on the fuel may be claimed with a fixed-scale charge applied to take account of private use. Alternatively – and you should tell your VAT Business Advice Centre if you intend to do this – no input tax is claimed and the fixed-scale charge is ignored. As a guide, claiming input tax and using the fixed-scale charge is normally the better way if private motoring paid for by the business is more than about 8,000 miles a year.

The quarterly scale charges are as follows:

| Engine Size | Diesel | | Petrol | |
| | Scale Charge | VAT | Scale Charge | VAT |
cc	£	£	£	£
1400 or less	225	33.51	242	36.04
1401 to 2000	225	33.51	307	45.72
Over 2000	286	42.59	453	67.46

Input tax on repairs and maintenance of business cars can be claimed whichever way you decide to deal with motor fuel.

Special schemes for retailers

Retailers often sell a mixture of both positive- and zero-rated goods but do not know how much of each from day to day. When this happens they can use one of the schemes devised to help them work out their VAT liabilities. If your business falls into this category you should study the leaflets telling you about the various schemes so that you do not pay too much tax.

Where retailers sell only goods which are liable to the standard rate of 17.5%, the amount of tax included in the gross takings for a period is $7/47$. Referred to as the 'VAT fraction', the basis for this calculation is as follows:

	£
Tax exclusive value (say)	100.00
Add: VAT @ 17.5%	17.50
Tax inclusive price	£117.50

The VAT included in the tax inclusive price is therefore:

$$\frac{17.5}{117.5} = \frac{7}{47}$$

For goods liable at 5% the 'VAT fraction' will be $1/21$. When retailers are asked for one, they must issue a proper tax invoice for supplies where the value exceeds £250. For supplies below this figure, till receipts will usually have enough information on them for the appropriate VAT fraction to be applied by customers who, in the course of their business, make retail purchases and want to claim back the input tax suffered.

Helpful schemes for smaller businesses

(a) The Flat Rate Scheme (FRS)

This has been designed particularly for businesses with an annual turnover level below £150,000 which do not want to spend too much time and effort dealing with the administrative complications of normal VAT accounting. Approval to use the FRS means that, although VAT can be charged to customers at the rate appropriate to the supplies a business makes, when VAT Returns have to be completed the tax can be accounted for at a fixed percentage of all income. The percentages are set by Customs according to the principal activity of the business: they are calculated in such a way that input tax on normal purchases is not claimed. Analysing purchase invoices between the net amounts and VAT is done away with and, coupled with Annual Accounting (see (b) below), the cost of record-keeping is cut at a time when business growth is often much more important.

Businesses are being strongly encouraged by Customs to use the FRS – so much so that an additional first year 1% reduction in the percentages is available to new businesses that register when they should and, at the same time, apply to use the FRS.

The FRS will not, however, suit all businesses. Those that make supplies to overseas customers and/or where VAT does not otherwise have to be charged at the standard rate will, in particular, have to look closely at whether the benefits the scheme offers outweigh the VAT which will have to be paid under the FRS based on all income. The loss in claiming input tax has, in particular, to be borne in mind. Any other available simplification methods will also have to be considered if turnover exceeds £187,500 and it looks as if it will stay at a level above the threshold of £150,000.

(b) Cash Accounting and Annual Accounting

These schemes are optional and aimed mainly at businesses with a turnover below £600,000, although there is some leeway if this threshold is temporarily exceeded for a special reason. Cash Accounting means that liabilities are geared to monies moving through a business. Using Annual Accounting, as the name implies, only one VAT Return has to be completed each year although there may be a requirement to make payments on account during the course of the year.

If they want to, new businesses with a turnover below £150,000 can apply to use Annual Accounting as well as the FRS (see (a) above) when they register for VAT. Although 'on account' VAT payments may be required, the FRS does automatically lead to the payment of VAT Return liabilities according to how much income is received. Where businesses have a turnover exceeding £150,000 they will normally need to have been up and running for a year and have established a history of complying with the VAT rules and regulations before they can qualify for Annual Accounting.

Apart from only having to submit one VAT Return each year, there are other benefits from Annual Accounting, including:

- fewer declarations, therefore fewer deadlines and less risk of penalties;

- a reduction of some paperwork during the year, with an extra month to complete the annual return; and

- fixed interim payments that provide an aid to cash flow planning.

(c) Second-hand goods schemes

For many years there have been a number of schemes where certain types of business have had to keep detailed stock records. Using the 'VAT fraction' they have had to work out the tax to pay on an item-by-item basis according to how much the selling price exceeds the purchase price. In this way, the liability is just on the dealer's margin, no allowance being made if an item is sold at a loss. There is also a Global Accounting Scheme which makes it much easier for those businesses trading in large volumes of second-hand low-value goods to work out the tax. Although a values limit of £500 for an article has been set, a business which uses this scheme can take the overall margin in the whole of the tax period and apply the VAT fraction to it. An item-by-item calculation is unnecessary.

Bad debts

Non-payment of bills can cause a lot of concern for businesses unable to use the FRS or Cash Accounting when working out their VAT Return liabilities. If output tax has been accounted for in previous VAT Returns but a customer has not made payment, it is only when the debt is more than 6 months old that an adjustment can be made to reduce the tax payable in a later period. The other side of the coin is that, for purchases where input tax has been claimed but a supplier's account has not been settled when 6 months have gone by, the input tax has to be paid back to Customs. Bad debt adjustments, although not separately shown on VAT Returns, have to be recorded separately in the VAT Account of the business. Listings have to be kept to support the entries, and further adjustments made to reflect any payments received, or made, later on.

Partial exemption

This is a complex area which occurs when some supplies made by a business are taxable, whether at a positive or the zero rate, and others are exempt. Strictly, the input tax may only be claimed when it relates to taxable supplies, but this is not always so. A relaxation in the rules allows recovery of all claimable input tax if that which relates to the exempt supplies is less than both £625 per month on average and 50% of the total input tax. The calculations for this have to be done when each VAT Return is completed. An annual adjustment is then carried out to iron out any peaks and troughs that occurred during the year.

Routine compliance checks

Customs have to make sure that businesses are accounting correctly for VAT. Your VAT Business Advice Centre may invite you to complete a questionnaire and ask for a copy of the most recent annual accounts that have been prepared. Alternatively an officer will arrange to come along and see you. At a visit, the officer will initially want to talk to you and ask questions about your business. This is followed by an examination of your books and records to make sure that you are keeping proper records and correctly dealing with your VAT Returns. The officer will draw your attention to any mistakes which he finds and issue an assessment for any underdeclared or overdeclared tax. Since assessments may span the three years prior to the visit, it is worthwhile reviewing beforehand, as a precautionary measure, the Returns that you have submitted. Misdeclaration penalties and default interest may be imposed if substantial amounts of tax are found to have been underdeclared.

Penalties, surcharges and interest

There are a number of penalties for businesses that are not careful with their VAT records, declarations and payments. Whenever Returns are submitted, the aim should be for the true tax in each and every period to be declared and paid. Getting it right first time is best for everybody's sake. Errors, although they may be innocent, are always possible. If, when you are preparing a Return for a current period, you find you have made mistakes in preceding quarters, you may be able to make an appropriate adjustment without incurring a penalty.

Any errors that, taken altogether, involve an amount of tax less than £2,000 can be adjusted in the Return for a current quarter. However, if the total of any errors exceeds £2,000, spotting where they have been made and what they amount to, and owning up, means that the chance of incurring the misdeclaration penalty may be avoided. Form VAT 652 is available for notifying your VAT Business Advice Centre of errors greater than £2,000. Alternatively, details of any errors of this size may be set out in a letter which should be sent to your VAT Business Advice Centre, together with a payment to correct the overall position. Default interest will normally be charged when assessments for errors are issued.

At the present time the level of the misdeclaration penalty is a flat 15% but whether or not it is imposed depends very much upon the correct amounts of output and input tax that should have been declared for the period.

A further type of penalty may also apply if mistakes are persistently made although, as with other penalties, it may be possible to get it reduced.

Failure to file VAT returns with the VAT Central Unit at Southend-on-Sea and/or pay the proper amount of tax when it is due can lead to the imposition of surcharges. These can range from 2% to 15% if a history of default builds up. Surcharge assessments will, however, seldom be issued unless calculated to exceed £400.

Supplies to/from EU countries

There are special rules for these supplies which, although they may differ from rules covering exports to, and imports from, countries outside the EU, have been designed to help businesses that trade with other member states. Normally, supplies of goods passing between the UK and businesses elsewhere in the EU can be zero-rated provided that the VAT Registration particulars of both parties feature on the invoices. Declarations apart from just the VAT Returns may have to be completed and it is as well to study carefully the appropriate leaflets issued by Customs if your business is likely to be involved with such supplies. How international supplies of services should be dealt with is particularly complicated.

Appeals

If you disagree with an officer's assessment or wish to appeal against a penalty or surcharge, you can ask for the matter to be reconsidered. A review should be carried out by someone at your VAT Business Advice Centre other than the officer who issued the assessment or penalty. Alternatively, an appeal can be lodged for hearing before an independent VAT Tribunal. Lodging an appeal does not prevent you from continuing to discuss or correspond with Customs in the hope that a settlement can be agreed without the need for a Tribunal hearing.

The outcome of Tribunal appeals depends very much upon the reasons why mistakes were made in the first place. Innocence is not normally accepted as an excuse.

Complaints

Standards have been laid down and all Customs officers are expected to abide by them. If you ever feel dissatisfied with the way your business affairs have been handled or that an officer has overstepped the mark and exceeded his authority, you can write to the person who is in overall charge of the VAT Business Centre or directly to the Complaints Unit for the area where your business is situated. The NAS will provide you with the address. Failure to resolve complaints can be followed up by contacting the Adjudicator's Office, which is the independent body set up specifically for this purpose.

Customs officers are committed to the same standards as the Inland Revenue – see the Service Commitment reproduced in Chapter 1.

6 THE SELF-EMPLOYED

You cannot simply choose to be taxed as a self-employed person. It is a matter of fact whether you are working on your own account. The concept of self-employment extends to all trades, professions and vocations. You are not self-employed if you are running your business through a company.

If you are employed but have some other freelance business activity as well, you will be taxed on these profits as a self-employed person.

Am I self-employed?

The main distinction between self-employed status and working as an employee is the lack of any 'master–servant' relationship. Sometimes it is difficult to distinguish the dividing line between an employment (a contract for service) and self-employment (a contract for services). You are likely to be classified as working on your own account if you:

- Are paid a fee, rather than a fixed hourly rate.
- Have no entitlement to paid holidays or sick leave.
- Do not receive any perks or benefits such as membership of a company pension plan.
- Are responsible for any losses arising out of your services.
- Can dictate how, when and where the work should be undertaken.
- Provide your own tools.

It is not necessary to formalize any business relationship by entering into a formal contract for the supply of your services. Nevertheless, having a contract makes sound business sense because it can deal with matters other than just the tax aspects of the relationship.

Starting up in business

Once you have set yourself up in business you must then come to grips with what you need to do about tax, National Insurance (see Chapter 7) and maybe Value Added Tax (see Chapter 5). I recommend you telephone the Inland Revenue on 08459 15 45 15 and ask for a copy of their booklet *Starting up in Business*. It will help you with what you need to know about keeping proper records as well as dealing with other matters relevant to your new self-employment. The booklet comes with Form CWF1 which you need to complete to register for tax and National Insurance. If you fail to notify the Inland Revenue that you have started up in business within three months after the end of the month in which you commenced your self-employment, you will be liable to a fixed penalty of £100.

Records

Under Self-Assessment there is a particular requirement for keeping proper records of all business transactions. The records you should maintain will depend upon the type and size of your business. You are, however, expected to record all of the following:

- sales and other business receipts as they come in, and you should retain the back-up records (for example, invoices, bank statements and paying-in slips to show where the income came from);

- purchases and other expenses for which, wherever possible, you should retain invoices for the goods acquired or costs incurred;

- purchases and sales of assets used in your business;

- amounts taken out of the business for personal use (drawings) and all monies paid into your business from personal funds (capital introduced).

For most businesses it is also good practice to maintain a separate bank account for the business and keep the following books of account, either manually or on computer:

- a cash book which summarizes and analyses all the entries in the bank account;

- a petty cash book to record all small cash transactions.

If you run a larger business you may well need to keep other books of account as well. No matter how large or small your business you would be well advised to keep your accounting records up to date.

You will have to retain your records for five years from the latest date by which your Tax Return has to be filed. For example, your completed Tax

Return for the year to 5 April 2004 must be sent back to your tax office by no later than 31 January 2005. It follows that your records for that year must be retained until 31 January 2010.

Accounts

At the end of each financial year all your transactions are brought together into an account of the income and expenditure of the business. Whenever possible a balance sheet should be drawn up showing the assets and liabilities of the business at the year-end.

You can choose the date to which you draw up the accounts of your trade or business each year. For this reason it is unlikely that the first set of accounts will cover a full year's business activities. You can make up your accounts from the date you start in business to the end of:

- A particular month.

- Your first year's trading.

- The calendar year on 31 December.

- The tax year on 5 April.

If your business is a seasonal one it may be a good idea to pick an annual accounting date to coincide with a slack time of the year and when stocks are low. Thereafter you should continue to draw up your accounts to the same date every year, although you can alter this where you can show good reason for a change.

You should also keep in mind that nowadays annual accounts of a business may well be needed for reasons other than tax. For example, your bank manager may want to see your accounts when weighing up an application for a business loan or overdraft facility.

Your accounts should be drawn up to show the profit or loss earned in the financial year. This is not usually the simple difference between the cash received and the cash paid out. For example, if you sell to some of your customers on credit there will inevitably be some unpaid invoices at the end of the financial year. Nevertheless, the amount of these outstanding invoices needs to come into your accounts as income for that period. Equally, where amounts are owing to your suppliers at the year-end these must be brought into the accounts as expenses incurred in the year. If your trade is one where you need to keep a stock of raw materials or finished goods, the value of that stock at the year-end must enter your accounts. It will usually be valued at cost or, in the case of redundant or old stock, at realizable value.

Make sure you include in your accounts all the expenses of running your business. If, for example, you are a married man and your wife helps you by taking telephone messages or acting as your part-time assistant or secretary, pay her a proper wage for these services. What you pay her can count as an expense in your accounts. She can then set off her personal allowance against her wages. If these are less than £4,615 a year there will be no tax or National Insurance to pay on them. There will be some items of expenditure, such as a car used both privately and in your business, when it will be difficult to differentiate precisely between the private and business elements of the expenditure. Where there is this overlap you should agree the proportion which relates to your business with the Inland Revenue. If you do your office work from home you can include as a deduction in your accounts a proportion of your home expenses, such as light, heat and insurance. Remember that if part of your home is used exclusively for business purposes, then should you come to sell your house the profit on sale attributable to that part will not be exempt from Capital Gains Tax.

Bob Lancaster is a printer by trade. He operates his business from a rented factory on an industrial estate. His wife keeps his accounts, prepares his VAT returns and acts as part-time secretary.

Bob started up in business in June 1997. He makes up his accounts to 31 October each year. The statement of his business income and expenses for the financial year to 31 October 2003 is as follows:

BOB LANCASTER – PRINTER

Profit and Loss Account for the year ended 31 October 2003

	£	£	£
Sales			267,800
Less: Cost of sales			
Stock of paper and other materials at start of year		3,400	
Purchases during the year		60,700	
		64,100	

Less:	Stock of paper and other		
	materials at end of year	3,800	
			60,300
Gross Profit			207,500
Less:	Overhead expenses		
	Wages and salaries	94,700	
	Factory expenses		
	Rent and rates	17,840	
	Light and heat	4,040	
	Cleaning	810	
	Insurance	1,310	
	Roof repairs	1,880	
	–	25,880	
	Secretarial assistance	4,000	
	Printing, postage and stationery	920	
	Telephone	1,360	
	Advertising and promotion	2,900	
	Travelling	1,140	
	Entertaining	390	
	Accountancy	1,850	
	Legal Fees – new lease	730	
	Car expenses		
	Road Fund Licence		
	and Insurance	880	
	Petrol and oil	1,270	
	Repairs and servicing	410	
		2,560	
	Business proportion 75%	1,920	
	Use of home as office ($1/7 \times 1{,}610$)	230	
	Home telephone (25%)	360	
	Bank interest and charges	4,280	
	Provision for bad debts (10% x 21,300)	2,130	
	Miscellaneous expenses	710	
			143,500
Profit for the year			**£64,000**

Standard accounting information

If at any time during the 2003/04 tax year you were in business then you will need to fill in the self-employment pages of your Tax Return for that year. For those in business with a turnover of more than £15,000 there is now a set format, as part of the self-employment pages of the Return, for reporting the annual income and expenses of your business. If accounts are not presented in the required format the Return will not be accepted as complete.

When Bob Lancaster, the printer, comes to complete the self-employment pages of his Tax Return for the year ended 5 April 2004 he will fill in the section on business income and expenses for his financial year to 31 October 2003 as follows:

	£	£	£
Sales/business income (excluding VAT)			267,800
Less: Cost of sales	60,300		
Other direct costs	—		
			60,300
Gross profit			207,500
Other income/profits			—
			207,500
Less: Expenses			
Employee costs	98,700		
Premises costs	24,230		
Repairs	1,880		
General administrative expenses	2,640		
Motor expenses	1,920		
Travel and subsistence	1,140		
Advertising, promotion and entertainment	3,290		
Legal and professional costs	2,580		
Bad debts	2,130		
Interest	4,280		
Other finance charges	—		
Depreciation and loss/(profit) on sale	—		
Other expenses	710		

Total expenses	143,500
Net profit	£64,000

Notes:	£
(1) Employee costs are:	
Wages and salaries	94,700
Wife's salary	4,000
	£98,700
(2) Premises costs are:	
Factory – rent and rates	17,840
Factory – light and heat	4,040
Factory – insurance	1,310
Factory – cleaning	810
Use of home as office	230
	£24,230
(3) General administrative expenses are:	
Printing, postage and stationery	920
Telephone (factory and home)	1,720
	2,640
(4) Legal and professional costs are:	
Accountancy	1,850
Legal fees	730
	£2,580

In order to minimize the risk of an Inland Revenue enquiry into your business accounts and Tax Return, it is important that the analysis of your business expenses over the various headings in the standardized accounting format follows a consistent pattern from year to year.

If the total annual turnover of your business is below £15,000 you can fill in the special, shortened income and expenses section in the self-employment pages of the Return. This comprises a three-line statement of:

- turnover and other business receipts;
- business expenses allowable for tax;
- resulting profit or loss.

You should, of course, still keep proper business accounts and records in order that you can draw up the annual three-line statement accurately.

Adjustment of profits

It does not follow that the profit shown by your business accounts is the same as the one on which you pay tax. This is because some items of expenditure are specifically not deductible in computing your taxable business profits. Types of expenditure which come into this category are business entertainment, non-business charitable donations, general provisions and reserves, professional costs related to capital expenditure, and the cost of items of a capital, as opposed to revenue, nature.

Although Bob Lancaster's accounts for his financial year to 31 October 2003 show a profit of £64,000, his taxable profits are £67,250, as follows:

	£	£
Profit as per accounts		64,000
Add Disallowable expenses:		
General provision for bad debts	2,130	
Entertainment	390	
Legal fees for new lease	730	
		3,250
Profit as adjusted for tax purposes		£67,250

The current-year basis of taxation

Under the current-year basis of taxation, self-employed individuals are taxed on the profits made in the tax year. The profits shown by annual accounts drawn up to a date other than the end of the tax year – 'the basis period' – are regarded as those of the year to 5 April.

> The tax-adjusted profit of £67,250 of Bob Lancaster's printing business for the year to 31 October 2003 will be taxed in 2003/04.

For the first year of business the taxable profits will be limited to those arising in the period from commencement to 5 April. On cessation the profits for the final tax year will be those arising in the period from the end of the basis period taxed in the previous tax year.

Under these rules it is possible that some periods of account will feature for more than one tax year. However, over the lifetime of a business it is intended that the profits should be taxed in full, once and once only. Accordingly, any profits which are taxed more than once will be eligible for a special relief. Known as overlap relief, it will be given either when a business ceases or for any earlier tax year for which the basis period is longer than 12 months.

> James Gray started his business on 1 September 2003. His annual accounting date is 31 August. He makes the following profits:
>
> | | |
> |---|---|
> | Year to 31.08.2004 | £15,900 |
> | Year to 31.08.2005 | £19,200 |
>
> The taxable profits for the first three tax years are:
>
> | Tax Year | Basis Period | Taxable Profit £ |
> |---|---|---|
> | 2003/04 | 01.09.2003 to 05.04.2004 | 9,275 |
> | 2004/05 | Year to 31.08.2004 | 15,900 |
> | 2005/06 | Year to 31.08.2005 | 19,200 |

The business closes down on 30 April 2010. The taxable profit in the final period from 1 September 2009 to 30 April 2010 amounts to £12,000. The final tax year is 2010/11 when James will be taxable on:

		£
Taxable profit in final period		12,000
Less: Overlap	01.09.2003 to 05.04.2004	9,275
Net taxable amount		£2,725

Special rules apply when a business changes its accounting date. Apart from the first and last years of business the system aims to tax the profits of a 12-month period in each tax year.

Sheila Windows commenced her business on 1 October 2003. She draws up her first accounts to 30 September 2004 which disclose a profit of £19,000. She then changes her accounting date to 31 December 2005. The accounts for the 15-month period show a taxable profit of £15,000. Her basis periods and taxable profits for the opening years of her business are:

Tax Year	Basis Period	Taxable Profit
		£
2003/04	01.10.2003 to 05.04.2004	9,500
2004/05	Year to 30.09.2004	19,000

The overlap period is from 01.10.2003 to 05.04.2004:

2005/06	01.10.2004 to 31.12.2005	
	(15 months)	15,000
Less: Overlap	01.10.2003 to 31.12.2003	4,750
Net taxable amount		£10,250

The overlap period was one of six months. As the accounting period from 1 October 2004 to 31 December 2005 is 15 months, the overlap relief is three months. The amount deducted from the taxable profits for 2005/06 is half of the original overlap profit. A further three months of overlap relief is then available either when the business ceases or for any subsequent tax year when the basis period is longer than 12 months.

Post-cessation expenses

Tax relief is allowed on specific types of expense incurred after a business has ceased. Relief is available for payments made within seven years of the permanent discontinuance of the business. The types of expense which qualify for this form of relief are those closely related to the trading or professional activities while they were carried on. Included, for example, is relief for debts which subsequently proved to be irrecoverable.

The relief is given by setting the payments made against income for the same tax year. Any excess can be treated as a capital loss of the same year only. Any unrelieved post-cessation expenses cannot be carried back or forward against either income or capital gains.

Capital allowances

Although you cannot deduct expenditure on items of a capital nature directly from your business profits, you do receive what are known as capital allowances on the expenditure.

Amounts spent by small and medium-sized businesses (your business is almost certain to qualify) attract the following rates of allowance in the first year:

* 40% for expenditure on plant and machinery, but not motor cars;

* 100% where the investment is in information and communications technology. This enhanced rate of first year allowance applies to expenditure on computers, software and internet-enabled mobile phones and similar devices incurred in the period from 1 April 2000 to 31 March 2004.

* 100% for purchases of new low-emission cars for use by you or your employees in your business. To qualify for this relief, a car must be

first registered on or after 17 April 2002 and either emit not more than 120 gm/km CO_2 or be electrically propelled.

* 25% for other motor cars. For cars costing more than £12,000 there is a maximum allowance of £3,000.

In subsequent years, the balance of expenditure is written down on the reducing-balance basis at the rate of 25% p.a. For cars the maximum writing-down allowance is restricted to £3,000 in a year.

A separate 'pool' of expenditure must be maintained for each of the following different categories:

* plant and equipment, including motor vans, lorries and cars costing up to £12,000;

* each car bought for over £12,000;

* each asset used for both personal and business use;

* each asset with a short life expectancy.

Where an asset on which capital allowances have been given is sold, the proceeds of sale must come into the computation of capital allowances. This can sometimes lead to a further allowance where an asset is sold for less than its written-down value for tax purposes. Alternatively, if it fetches an amount greater than its written-down value this can often mean that part of the allowances already given needs to be withdrawn. These adjustments are respectively referred to as balancing allowances and balancing charges.

In his accounting year to 31 October 2003, our printer, Bob Lancaster, traded in his old car for £2,000 and bought a new car for £11,600. In June of the year he also spent £6,000 on a binding machine. His claim to capital allowances for 2003/04, based on his capital expenditure in the year to 31 October 2003, is:

	Pool	Car with Private Use
	£	£	£
Written-down values brought forward from 2002/03	3,260	2,640
Sale proceeds of car		2,000
Balancing allowance		640

Additions in the year:			
Binding machine		6,000	
New car			11,600
		―――	
		9,260	
Allowances due:			
First year – 40%	2,400		
Writing down – 25%	815	3,215	2,900
	―――	―――	―――
Carried forward to 2003/04		£6,045	£8,700
		≡≡≡	≡≡≡
Summary of allowances:			
First year		2,400	
Writing down		3,715	
Balancing		640	
		―――	
		6,755	
Less: 25% private use of car		885	
		―――	
2003/04 Capital allowances		£5,870	
		≡≡≡	

Capital allowances are treated as a trading expense of your business. Any balancing charges are added to your profit as a trading receipt. It follows that the chargeable period for the purposes of calculating your capital allowances is the same as that for which you draw up your accounts. This means that the amount of writing-down allowances to which you are entitled is determined by reference to the length of the period of account. Thus, if you draw up accounts for an eight-month period, $8/12$ of the writing-down allowances can be set against taxable profits for that period. Similarly, if a period of account extends to 15 months the tax deductible allowances are equivalent to $15/12$ of the writing-down allowances. In the event that a period of account exceeds 18 months it will be divided into one of 12 months and the balancing period with a restricted writing-down allowance.

Under Self-Assessment there is a section in the self-employment pages of your Tax Return for you to summarize your claim to capital allowances.

Losses

Most businesses cannot escape going through a bad spell at some stage in their existence. Where the results of your business for the year show a loss you will be able to claim tax relief on the loss as increased by any claim to capital allowances which count as trading expenses. You can elect to set a trading loss against other income for the same tax year, or the preceding year. You cannot claim relief for only part of a loss.

> Martin Peters has been in business for many years. He makes up his accounts to 30 November each year. He makes a loss in the year ended 30 November 2004 which can be claimed against his other income in 2004/05 and/or carried back and relieved against his total income in 2003/04.

Any unrelieved loss of your business must then be carried forward to be set against the profits from the same business in later years.

Otherwise you can claim to offset a trading loss against capital gains as follows:

- The claim is for relief on the amount of the trading loss which cannot be set against your other income in the year or on which tax relief has already been allowed in some other way.

- The maximum loss eligible for relief against capital gains is equivalent to the amount of your gains chargeable to Capital Gains Tax before taper relief is applied.

- It is not possible to make a partial claim.

- It is possible that personal allowances may be wasted as well as the annual exemption for Capital Gains Tax (see Chapter 12).

There is an alternative form of loss relief available for new businesses where:

- Losses incurred during the first four years of assessment are allowed to be set against your income in the three years prior to that in which the loss arises.

- Relief is first of all given against your income for the earliest year. For example, if you started out in business during 2003/04 and incurred a loss in the first period of trading, the proportion attributable to the tax year 2003/04 can be set off against your income in 2000/01, 2001/02 and 2002/03 , starting with 2000/01.

Frequently it is necessary to incur expenditure on a new business venture before it starts to trade. Any such expenditure incurred within seven years prior to the commencement of trade is treated as a separate loss sustained in the tax year in which trading began.

There is also a special form of loss relief for those businesses which incur a loss in their final period of trading. As the business has ceased there cannot be any future profits against which the loss might be relieved. Therefore, you are allowed to set a loss arising in the last 12 months of trading against the profits from the same business in the final tax year as well as the three preceding years, beginning with the profits of the last year and working backwards.

Ralph Collins retires from business on 30 November 2004. Apart from the final eight months when he loses £21,000 his business had always been successful. His recent taxable profits had been as follows:

Accounting Year		Taxable Profits £	Year of Charge
Year ended 31 March	2001	12,000	2000/01
Year " " "	2002	15,000	2001/02
Year " " "	2003	6,000	2002/03
Year " " "	2004	8,000	2003/04

The terminal loss can be set off as follows:

2003/04	8,000	leaving nil taxable profits
2002/03	6,000	leaving nil taxable profits
2001/02	7,000	reducing the taxable profits to £8,000
	£21,000	

The Enterprise Allowance

The Enterprise Allowance, or Business Start-Up Allowance, is a weekly flat rate payment to individuals leaving the unemployment register to set up in business. The allowance is not included in the takings of the recipient's business, although it is chargeable to Income Tax.

Taking on an employee

If you are thinking of taking on an assistant or an extra pair of hands for the first time, you should inform your tax office dealing with your business. They will immediately send the information to the right tax office since it is likely to be a different office to that dealing with your business. You should then receive a New Employer's Starter Pack containing all the instructions, tables and forms you will need.

As an employer you are responsible for:

- Working out the deductions for Income Tax (PAYE) and National Insurance Contributions from the salary or wage of your employees each pay day, whether this be weekly or monthly.

- Paying over the deductions to the Collector of Taxes each month. These payments can be made every quarter where your average monthly payments of tax and National Insurance Contributions are less than £1,500.

- Letting your tax office know every year how much each employee has earned and the deductions you have made for Income Tax and National Insurance Contributions. All the deductions should reconcile to the total of the amounts paid over to the Collector of Taxes. You must also give details of any benefits paid or provided.

- Giving your employees certificates showing their earnings for the tax year, deductions for Income Tax and National Insurance Contributions and the value of any benefits provided.

Foster carers

Beginning with 2003/04 there is a new relief for the self-employed who receive income from local authorities or independent fostering providers for providing foster care to children and young people.

There are two parts to the relief:

- An exemption from income tax on receipts which do not exceed the qualifying amount for any year;

- A simplified optional method of calculating taxable profits where receipts are more than the qualifying amount.

The annual qualifying amount is made up of two parts which must be added together. They are:

- a fixed amount for each household – £10,000 for 2003/04; and

- a weekly amount for each foster child placed with you – for 2003/04, £200 a week for a child under 11 years of age and £250 a week for a child over 11 years of age.

Mollie Ford, who lives on her own, provides foster care for two boys during 2003/04. The 12-year-old is only with her for 16 weeks but the 9-year-old boy stays with her for the whole year. Her qualifying amount for 2003/04 is £24,400 calculated as follows:

	£
Fixed amount	10,000
9-year-old (52 weeks x £200)	10,400
12-year-old (16 weeks x £250)	4,000
	———
2003/04 qualifying amount	£24,400

Where your receipts (fees, salaries, reward payments, allowances, etc.) exceed the annual qualifying amount you can choose between paying tax on:

- your actual profits from foster caring, worked out on the principles which apply for any other business; or

- profits worked out on a simplified method which is the difference between your total receipts for the year less the annual qualifying amount.

Whichever way you choose to be taxed, you must at least keep records of your receipts and the ages and number of weeks that you care for each child placed with you. For this purpose a week runs from Monday to the following Sunday. Part of a week counts as a full week.

Special situations

In the space available it has only been possible for me to paint a general picture of the way in which business profits are taxed. If you are a Lloyd's underwriter, a farmer, a writer or a subcontractor in the construction industry you should be aware that there are special rules which apply in calculating the tax on the profits from your trade or profession. In these and other situations it is advisable to seek professional assistance.

The letting of holiday accommodation in the UK is treated as a trade. The accommodation has to be furnished residential property that is available for renting by the public as holiday accommodation for at least 140 days during each tax year. It must actually be let for a minimum of 70 days. There are other requirements that also need to be satisfied. Capital gains on disposals of holiday accommodation falling within these rules qualify for the replacement and retirement reliefs which apply to business assets (see Chapter 12).

7 NATIONAL INSURANCE CONTRIBUTIONS, STATE SOCIAL SECURITY AND INSURED BENEFITS

Whether you are employed or self-employed, you will have to pay National Insurance Contributions, as well as Income Tax, by reference to your earnings or business profits. In turn, the payment of sufficient National Insurance Contributions makes you eligible to claim those Social Security benefits which are based on your contribution history. Many benefits, however, such as those payable to the Disabled, do not depend upon the payment of contributions.

National Insurance Contributions

There are four different types of contribution which are payable:

- Class 1 by employees;
- Class 2 by the self-employed;
- Class 3 which is voluntary;
- Class 4 by the self-employed, based on profits.

You will not be liable for contributions once you have retired and passed normal retirement age, which is currently 60 for a woman and 65 for a man, even if you carry on working for someone else or in your own business.

For National Insurance the earnings of employees on which Class 1 contributions are calculated include:

- a salary or wage – before deduction for pension contributions;
- overtime, bonuses and commission;
- holiday pay;
- statutory sick and maternity pay.

However, no contributions are payable by employees on benefits-in-kind.

Your contributions are usually worked out as a percentage of your weekly or monthly salary or wage, subject to lower and upper earnings limits. If you choose to have a break when moving jobs, or there is a period when you are unemployed, this has no effect on the contributions you will have to pay when you go back to work.

There are special rules for company directors. The contributions due from a company director are worked out on the basis that each tax year is an earnings period even if the director is paid monthly or leaves during the year.

If you have more than one employment you are liable for contributions on your earnings from all your employers. Nevertheless there is an over-all annual maximum limit of contributions payable by employees. Where the total amount of deductions for your National Insurance Con-tributions exceeds this annual limit then you should apply for a refund of the overpayment. Alternatively you can apply for deferment where you can envisage that the contributions which will be taken off your earnings from two or more employments are such that the total deduc-tions will exceed the maximum annual limit. To apply for deferment you will need to complete a Form CF379 before the beginning of the tax year when you want to defer the payment of contributions. The Contribu-tions Office of the Inland Revenue will then instruct one or other of your employers not to withhold contributions from your earnings. After the end of the tax year your overall contribution history for that year is reviewed. If, for some reason or another, insufficient contributions have been collected on the earnings from all employments then the Contri-butions Office will send you a calculation and demand for the balance due.

There are two rates of National Insurance Contributions payable by the self-employed. Class 2 is a weekly flat rate. You can pay by either direct debit every month or by quarterly bill every 13 weeks. If your earnings are below a specified annual limit you can be exempted from paying these contributions. You should apply in advance for small-earnings exception. Class 4 contributions are based on a percentage of your tax-able business profits, after capital allowances, but before relief for pension contributions. These are accounted for through the tax system along with the annual tax liability on your profits as a self-employed tax-payer.

In certain circumstances, for example where you are also in employment and paying Class 1 contributions, you can apply to defer payment of both Class 2 and Class 4 contributions.

The payment of Class 3 contributions is voluntary. An individual who is neither employed nor in self-employment can pay Class 3 contributions in order to preserve entitlement to the state pension on retirement.

The rates of National Insurance Contributions for 2003/04 are in Appendix 4 at the end of the book. Your nearest Inland Revenue (National Insurance Contributions) office will supply you with leaflets and forms relating to National Insurance contributions. Appendix 5 is a list of those leaflets with the widest application.

State Retirement Pensions

There are three types of state retirement pension:

* the basic retirement (or old person's) pension;

* a state earnings-related pension (SERPS/S2P);

* a graduated pension.

State retirement pensions are payable to men who have reached age 65 and to women aged 60, subject, of course, to their contribution history. The contribution requirements which you must meet before you are entitled to the basic state pension are:

* The payment of Class 1, 2 or 3 National Insurance Contributions in any one tax year since 6 April 1975 such as to make that year a qualifying year. This is one in which you have received qualifying earnings equivalent to at least 52 times the lower weekly earnings limit for National Insurance purposes for that year. Alternatively, you must actually have paid 50 flat-rate contributions at any time before 6 April 1975.

* The establishment of qualifying years for around 90% of your working life before you can receive the full basic pension. You need nine or ten qualifying years to get the minimum – 25% – basic pension payable.

As the name implies, the state second pension scheme (S2P) is dependent on your earnings. You can get this additional pension if in any tax year since April 1978 you have paid the standard rate of Class 1 National Insurance Contributions on earnings between the lower and upper earnings limits. Furthermore, each Class 2 Contribution paid by the self-employed counts as one week's earnings at the lower earnings limit applying in that year.

As well as being entitled to the basic and additional pensions, certain individuals will be entitled to a pension under the graduated scheme. This was in operation between April 1961 and April 1975.

In addition to the basic pension a man may receive extra pension for:

- a wife;

- dependent children;

- a woman looking after his children.

A married woman may benefit from a retirement pension in one or other of three distinct ways:

- on her own contribution record;

- based on her husband's contribution if she is over 60 and retired so long as her husband is receiving a basic retirement pension;

- as a wife dependent on her husband. He is then entitled to an increase in his pension.

The retirement pension payable to a widow will depend on whether she was widowed before the normal retirement age of 60 or was widowed afterwards.

Social Security Benefits

It is the Department for Work and Pensions (DWP) which is responsible for administering all aspects of the social security system. There are local DWP offices throughout the country. The framework of the social security system is now so substantial, and the range of benefits so wide and varied, it is only possible for me to give a brief summary of the main benefits.

Many benefits are only payable to individuals who have an established history of paying National Insurance Contributions. The type of benefit you can then claim depends on the nature of contributions paid as follows:

Type of Benefit	Class 1 (Employed)	Class 2 (Self-Employed)	Class 3 (Voluntary)
Retirement Pension			
— basic	Yes	Yes	Yes
— additional	Yes	No	No
— widow's	Yes	Yes	Yes
Bereavement allowance	Yes	Yes	Yes
Bereavement payment	Yes	Yes	Yes
Widowed parent's allowance	Yes	Yes	Yes
Widow's Payment	Yes	Yes	Yes
Incapacity benefit	Yes	Yes	No
Jobseeker's allowance	Yes	No	No
Statutory Sick and Maternity Pay	Yes	No	No

Other benefits do not depend upon the payment of contributions. Equally some benefits paid to you by the state are taxable, others are tax free.

To be able to claim either statutory sick or maternity pay you must be earning enough to pay Class 1 National Insurance Contributions. A woman will qualify for statutory maternity pay if she has been working for the same employer continuously for 26 weeks up to, and including, the 15th week before her baby is due. She must provide evidence of being pregnant and give her employer sufficient notice of leaving work. The benefit is payable for 26 weeks beginning not earlier than the 11th week before the baby is due although the woman can actually select the time over which she will be absent from work.

Statutory sick pay is a flat-rate cash payment made to employees by their employer. To be eligible to claim you must be both incapable of work and not actually do any work at all on the day in question. It is not payable for the first three agreed qualifying days in any period when you are too unwell to work. In any period of sickness you have a maximum entitlement to 28 weeks of statutory sick pay.

Fathers are allowed up to 2 weeks leave from work during the first 8 weeks of their child's life. Statutory paternity pay is also a flat-rate cash payment. The qualifying requirements are the same as those for statutory maternity pay.

Incapacity benefit is a benefit for individuals under state pension age, provided they have paid a qualifying amount of National Insurance Contributions, who are unable to work because of illness or disability. Employees will normally get statutory sick pay for the first 28 weeks of sickness before moving on to incapacity benefit at the short-term higher rate. There are three different rates of benefit and additional supplements which may be paid. Incapacity benefit is not means-tested, but it is taxable. Any tax due will be deducted directly from the benefit paid to claimants who do not have another source of income already subject to PAYE. Where claimants do have another source of income on which PAYE is applied – such as an occupational pension from a former employer – any tax due on the benefit will be collected by adjusting the tax code applied to the other income and deducting tax from that other income.

In order to claim the jobseeker's allowance an individual needs to satisfy a number of conditions. The main features of the jobseeker's allowance, which is taxable, are that:

- entitlement is based on either a satisfactory contribution record or a means-tested low income;

- it is a weekly benefit with supplements for age and other personal circumstances;

- it is payable to unemployed individuals between the ages of 18 and state pensionable age. A claimant must sign a jobseeker's agreement which sets out the steps he or she intends to take towards full-time employment.

An individual is disqualified from receiving benefit if he or she fails to honour the obligations of the jobseeker's agreement, or refuses to follow either recommendations or directions of the employment adviser.

Other benefits include:

- income support, which is a non-contributory weekly benefit paid to individuals who do not have sufficient money to live on. The needs of each claimant are assessed depending on their circumstances. However, claimants with savings and capital over £8,000 do not qualify for income support.

- child benefit, which is not means tested and is payable to individuals bringing up children. For couples who are married it is the wife who should make the claim. The benefit is payable for all children under 16 years old. Children over age 15, but under 19, still qualify provided they are still in full-time education which includes courses at school or college up to 'A' Level. Child benefit is not payable for children studying beyond this level – for example for a university degree.

- benefits for employees who suffer personal injury from an accident arising out of their employment. The injury can result in either physical or mental impairment.

- benefits for the disabled such as the attendance and invalid care allowances. The attendance allowance is targeted at individuals who are seriously disabled, mentally or physically, and who need a lot of care and attention. On the other hand the invalid care allowance is payable to those individuals who are unable to work because they have to look after a relative who is either sick or disabled.

All the social security benefits, distinguishing between those which are taxable and non-taxable, are listed in Appendix 6 at the end of the book. The rates of the main taxable social security benefits for 2003/04 are in Appendix 7.

Pension Credit

An individual is entitled to the Pension Credit if he or she:

- lives in Great Britain;

- satisfies at least one of two requirements of the guarantee and savings credits respectively;

- has reached the qualifying age.

The guarantee credit 'tops up' the income of a single claimant to £102.10 per week. For couples the weekly income limit increases to £155.80. A claimant's income includes:

- a state and any other pension;

- earnings;

- Social Security benefits;

- notional investment income of £1 a week for every £500 of savings or capital in excess of £6,000 (excluding your home and possessions).

The purpose of the savings credit, the rules for which are far from simple, is to reduce Pension Credit by 40% of the amount by which a pensioner's income exceeds the basic state pension.

The guarantee credit is available to both men and women who have reached age 60. The qualifying age for both men and women increases to age 65 for the savings credit.

Insured benefits

Benefits paid under insurance policies that provide against financial loss caused by unemployment, accident, sickness disability or infirmity are not taxable. The different types of insurance policy with tax-free benefits are:

- mortgage payment protection insurance: these provide income to meet mortgage commitments in the event of accident, sickness, disability or unemployment;

- permanent health insurance: these provide continuing income in the event of accident, sickness or disability;

- creditor insurance: these provide benefits to meet existing obligations and commitments, such as loans and domestic utility bills;

- certain kinds of long-term care insurance: that is those which provide benefits to meet the cost of the provision of care in the event of accident, sickness, disability or infirmity but only where policies are taken out before the need for care becomes apparent.

8 PERSONAL PENSIONS

Wherever possible I imagine you will want to avoid a drop in your living standards when you come to retire and will be looking to your pension plan to replace, at the very least, some part of your previous earnings or business profits. To give you the best possible opportunity of building up a worthwhile pension, to supplement your entitlement to the State Pension, you should start contributing to an appropriate plan as soon as you can reasonably afford to do so.

Many employers, particularly large organizations, have long-established Company Pension Schemes and have been offering employees membership of their schemes for a considerable number of years. If you are employed by such an organization you should satisfy the requirements to join their pension scheme. Some employers do not require their employees to make any contributions towards their benefits on retirement. In other cases employees must contribute a percentage of their annual salary in addition to the amount that their employer pays into their schemes each year.

Employers with 5 or more employees (including directors) must provide their employees with access to a designated Stakeholder Pension Scheme, or offer a satisfactory alternative. Although such employers must offer a Stakeholder Pension Scheme there is no requirement that they need contribute nor are employees bound to join the scheme.

If your employer has not set up his own scheme for his employees or you are self-employed you will need to make your own personal pension arrangements.

Eligible individuals

To be eligible to take out a personal pension plan you must be resident and ordinarily resident in the UK for at least part of a tax year. You can do so if:

- you are self-employed;

- you are in employment. You can choose to opt out of your

employer's own company scheme and take out a personal pension plan instead. Your employer can make contributions into your personal pension plan in addition to the amount of premiums you pay into the plan;

- you opt out of the state earnings-related pension scheme (S2P). The Department of Work and Pensions will then pay the difference between the full and reduced rates of National Insurance Contributions into your personal pension scheme. Opting out of SERPS does not affect your entitlement to the basic State Pension.

- you are neither employed nor self-employed. In such circumstances the maximum contribution limit is £3,600 (gross) per annum.

Benefits on retirement

When you start making regular monthly or annual contributions into a personal pension plan do remember you cannot benefit from the funds building up in your plan until you come to retire and draw your pension. Throughout this period your contributions will be invested in a tax-free fund. As we will see later on in this chapter you will also receive tax relief on your premiums. You benefit from a further tax concession on retirement when 25% of the value of the fund built up in your personal pension plan can be paid to you as a tax-free lump sum. The remainder of your fund is used to provide a pension which will be payable throughout the rest of your life. You can even arrange for this to be paid for a minimum guaranteed period, usually five years, should you die within this period. It is also possible to provide for a dependant's pension if you die before your spouse. As we will see in Chapter 10 the pension you eventually come to draw from your scheme is taxable.

The tax-free lump sum and pension can be taken at any time between the ages of 50 and 75. You do not actually need to retire before taking your pension. The Inland Revenue has approved earlier retirement ages of 30, 35, 40 or 45 for some professions and occupations, particularly in professional sport; for example, footballers can retire at age 35 and take maximum benefits. Those benefits within your plan which were purchased through opting out of S2P cannot be drawn until you reach normal state retirement age.

If unfortunately you die before retirement a lump sum, depending on the terms of your particular plan, will probably be refundable. This can be paid out to beneficiaries nominated by you during your lifetime or, alternatively, to your executors. Any lump sum payable is free of tax.

Deferred annuities

Holders of personal pension plans can defer, if they wish, the purchase of their annuity up to age 75. In the meantime, during the deferral period, they can make income withdrawals taxable under PAYE in the same way as annuities. There is a set formula for working out the maximum amount of income withdrawal, which must be reviewed every three years.

During the period of deferral, the pension fund remains tax free and protected from Inheritance Tax. However, no further contributions can then be made into the plan.

Should the personal pension plan holder die after benefits have been taken from the plan, but before the annuity has been purchased, a surviving spouse or dependant has three options:

- for the time being to continue making income withdrawals. The annuity can be purchased either on the deceased's 75th birthday or his or her own 75th birthday, whichever is the earlier;

- to purchase an annuity immediately;

- to take the fund in cash, when there will be a special 35% tax charge on the value of the fund.

Tax relief on premiums

All contributions into personal pension plans are paid after deduction of tax at the basic rate – currently 22%. Should you be liable to tax at the higher rate of 40%, and be in employment, you will need to tell your tax office about your personal pension plan so that the extra tax relief on your premiums over and above that due at the basic rate can be allowed in your code number. Other taxpayers can claim their higher rate tax relief as part of their annual self-assessment.

Annual premiums in excess of £3,600 gross can only be paid based on earnings. For:

- employees, earnings include the annual amount of taxable benefits-in-kind.

- the self-employed, earnings are the annual taxable business profits as reduced by capital allowances and any losses.

The most you can contribute each year is expressed as a percentage of your earnings and depends on your age. Furthermore, there is a maximum earnings limit on which the percentage limit can be calculated. For 2003/04 this is £99,000. It increases each year in line with the movement in the Retail Prices Index. The contribution limits are as follows:

Age at Start of Tax Year	Percentage Limit of Earnings
Under 36	17.5
36–45	20
46–50	25
51–55	30
56–60	35
Over 60	40

The maximum pension contributions payable can be based on the appropriate percentage of the higher of an individual's net relevant earnings for:

- that tax year, or

- in any of the five preceding tax years.

This rule will be of particular help for those in self-employment whose profits often fluctuate from one year to the next.

Up to 10% of your annual premiums can be paid into a policy providing for the payment of a lump sum to your dependants in the event of your death before the age of 75.

Premiums paid in the year can either be deducted from your taxable income in the year of payment, or alternatively you can elect for them to be treated as if paid in the preceding year provided you do not exceed the contribution limit for the earlier year. Premiums carried back to the previous tax year must be paid before 31 January following the end of the tax year. The election to carry back the tax relief to the previous year must be made on or before the date of payment of the premiums.

Retirement annuities

Personal pension schemes, in one form or another, have been around since the beginning of July 1988. Up to that date the self-employed and employees who were not members of their employer's own pension schemes could take out retirement annuities. No new retirement annuities may now be taken out although you can continue to pay regular and single premiums into existing contracts. Retirement annuities differ from personal pension plans in a number of ways:

- employers are not allowed to make contributions into them;

- although there is no maximum earnings limit on which premiums may be paid, the contribution limits are not so generous:

Age at Start of Tax Year	Percentage Limit of Earnings
Under 51	17.5
51–55	20.0
56–60	22.5
Over 60	27.5

- you cannot draw your benefits before age 60. It is possible to transfer the benefits under a retirement annuity to a personal pension in order to draw down the tax-free lump sum and pension before age 60;

- if you are in employment you cannot pay your premiums after the deduction at source of tax at the basic rate;

- the method of calculating the maximum amount of the tax-free lump sum on retirement is more generous;

- where you do not pay premiums up to the maximum permissible amount in any year the shortfall can be carried forward for up to six years. Relief outstanding for earlier years is used up before that still available for later years.

Peter Wong has been in business for many years. Since 1999/2000 Peter has not been making the maximum contributions into his retirement annuity contract as follows:

Tax Year	Premiums Paid £	Maximum Permissible £	Shortfall £
1999/2000	1,300	2,400	1,100
2000/01	1,400	1,800	400
2001/02	1,000	2,000	1,000
2002/03	1,500	2,300	800

During 2003/04 Peter paid premiums of £5,000; the maximum permissible premium limit for the year was only £2,000. Nevertheless relief will be given for £5,000, as follows:

	£	£
Premium limit for 2003/04		2,000
Unused relief:		
1999/2000	1,100	
2000/01	400	
2001/02	1,000	
2002/03 (part)	500	
	——	3,000
2003/04 Pension premium relief		£5,000

Personal pension planning

If you are still contributing into a retirement annuity you will often have to decide between continuing with this policy or instead opting to take out a personal pension plan. Where your salary or profits fall short of the earnings 'cap' of £99,000 you should consider contributing as much as you can into an existing retirement annuity as well as taking advantage of the higher contribution limits for personal pensions.

John Wallace aged 44 earns £54,000 per annum. He has an existing retirement annuity and pays premiums of £5,200 each year.

John's maximum contribution limits are:

(1)   Into his retirement annuity – £9,450 (17.5% x £54,000)

(2)   Into a personal pension – £10,800 (20% x £54,000)

John can pay either:

(a)   A further £4,250 into his retirement annuity and contribute £1,350 into a personal pension, or

(b)   A premium of £5,600 into a personal pension.

If you earn more than the amounts in the following table you should consider paying the maximum premiums into your retirement annuity.

Age at 6 April 2003	Earnings (£)
Under 36	99,000
36–45	113,142
46–50	141,429
51–55	148,500
56–60	154,000
Over 60	144,000

Veronica Adams aged 48 earns £150,000 per annum. She has an existing retirement annuity and contributes £12,000 each year.

Veronica's maximum contribution limits are:

(1)   Into her retirement annuity – £26,250 (17.5% x £150,000)

(2)   Into a personal pension – £24,750 (25% x £99,000)

Veronica can either contribute:

(a)   A further £14,250 into her retirement annuity, or

(b)   A premium into a personal pension plan. If she chooses to do so the total additional contributions she can make into the new personal pension and her existing retirement annuity between them are £12,750.

If your earnings are below the amounts in the above table you should again contribute the maximum amount into your existing retirement annuity and top this up by paying a further premium into a personal pension plan.

Alan Potter aged 57 earns £110,000 per annum. He has a retirement annuity and pays premiums of £13,000 annually.

Alan's maximum contribution limits are:

(1) Into his retirement annuity – £24,750 (22.5% x £110,000)

(2) Into a personal pension – £34,650 (35% x £99,000)

Alan can either contribute:

(a) A further £11,750 into his retirement annuity and pay a personal pension premium of £9,900, or

(b) An amount of £21,650 into a personal pension.

9 INVESTMENT INCOME

Most of you will at some time or other need to look into the various types of investment on offer. Perhaps you will be looking to find a suitable home for regular savings or to invest a more substantial amount such as an inheritance or a lump sum on retirement. Investment or unearned income is that which does not depend on your active involvement or physical effort in some business or trade. Bank or building society interest, dividends on shares or unit trust holdings, rents, income from a trust and interest on government stocks are all investment income.

Tax-free income

The most widely known investments where the return is free of both Income Tax and Capital Gains Tax are some of those available from National Savings and Investments. They are:

- Fixed-Interest and Index-linked Savings Certificates;
- Premium Bond prizes;

Also tax free is:

- interest on your TESSA, provided you do not touch the capital;
- income from your PEP and ISA investments;
- dividends you receive on shares you own in Venture Capital Trusts.

No details of these need to be shown on your annual Income Tax Return.

Rental income

The letting of property, including isolated or casual lettings, is treated as a business for tax purposes. This applies to a flat, house, shop or any other property that you let out to tenants. Most of the rules currently in force for working out the taxable profits from a trade or profession also apply in calculating your annual profits from let property. All income from property situated in the United Kingdom is pooled together, regardless of the type of lease. It does not matter whether the property is furnished or unfurnished. Losses from your business of renting out property can be carried forward to be set against future profits of your income from the property business.

Apart from expenditure of a capital nature, such as that on structural alterations or improvements, the general running costs of a property can be set against rental income. Allowable expenses include:

- amounts spent on letting out the property including estate agents' fees, advertising expenses and the costs of drawing up an inventory;

- interest relating to your property letting business. It matters not whether the interest is payable on a loan or overdraft;

- rent collection costs;

- maintenance, repairs and redecorations;

- premiums on buildings and contents insurance policies;

- rent and water rates;

- Council Tax that you pay for your tenants;

- all other expenses of managing the property such as stationery, postage, etc.;

- your share of expenditure on the common parts of the let property.

Karen Donnelly owns a flat which she lets out to tenants during 2003/04. The rental income for the year amounts to £12,813 as follows:

		£	£
Rent receivable from let property			18,000
Less:	Expenses		
	Rent collection costs	2,115	
	Council Tax	620	
	Service charges	860	
	Water rates	210	
	Building insurance premium	290	
	Roof repairs	752	
	Garden maintenance	340	
			5,187
2003/04 net rental income			£12,813

If your gross rental income before expenses is less than £15,000 in the year, you do not need to list the expenses separately. The total expenses can be entered on your Return as one amount.

Where you are renting out property which is unfurnished, you can claim capital allowances on the cost of fixtures, fittings and equipment incurred on the let property.

If you are letting a furnished property you can claim an additional deduction to cover the cost of wear and tear to furnishings and fittings. This can be what you actually spend on renewing fixtures and fittings. Alternatively you can claim a fixed allowance of 10% of the rent less amounts paid out on water rates and Council Tax. If Karen's flat in the preceding illustration had been let furnished this allowance would be £1,144 as follows:

	£
Rent receivable	18,000
Less: Water rates and Council Tax	830
	£17,170
Wear and tear allowance: 10%	£1,717

The rules dealing with the taxation of premiums on leases are more complicated and outside the scope of this book.

Rent-a-Room

Income from the furnished letting of spare rooms in your home is tax-free provided the annual gross rents do not exceed £4,250 per annum. The space you let out must be in your only or main home. This can be a house, flat, caravan or even a houseboat. You can elect to opt out of the special form of relief. You will then be taxed under the normal rules dealing with income from furnished lettings. If, for example, there was a loss on the letting which could be set against other income then it would pay you to make the opt-out election.

Where your annual gross rents are more than £4,250 you can choose to pay tax on the excess gross rents, without any relief for expenses, or under the rules for taxing furnished lettings income.

> Theresa Stevens, who is a basic rate taxpayer, lets a room in her house for £4,800 per annum.
>
> The expenses that can be set against the income total £1,400. Under the Rent-a-Room relief her Income Tax liability is £121.00 (£4,800 – £4,250) x 22%. Alternatively, under the normal rules, the tax liability would total £748 (£4,800 – £1,400) x 22%.

It is necessary to make an election if you want to adopt the simple method of paying Income Tax on the gross rents over £4,250 per annum.

Where an individual and some other person are entitled to income under the Rent-a-Room scheme the £4,250 limit is halved. Each lessor's exempt amount is then £2,125. This rule means that a married couple taking in lodgers should be able to arrange their affairs in such a way that the letting income is divisible between them (each spouse will then have a limit of £2,125); or goes wholly to either husband or wife (in which case either spouse will be due the full £4,250 limit).

Dividends and interest

The tables below set out the types of investment where the dividends and interest are paid to the investor:

- with a non-repayable tax credit;
- after deduction of Income Tax;
- no tax deducted.

Tax credit of 10%

Dividends on shares

Income distributions on unit trust holdings

Savings Income – Tax deducted at 20%

Building society interest

*Interest on British Government stocks, with some exceptions

Bank deposit interest

National Savings Fixed Rate Savings Bonds

Purchased life annuities – income element

Savings Income – Interest not taxed at source

*Interest on British Government stocks

National Savings investment accounts

National Savings Income and Capital Bonds

National Savings Pensioners' Bonds

Certificates of Tax Deposit

Single deposits over £50,000 for a fixed period of not more than five years

Deposits with non-UK branches of banks and building societies

* You can receive interest on your investments in British Government stocks without tax of 20% deducted at source. However, if you are receiving your interest after deduction of tax, and you want your interest to be paid to you before tax in future, you will have to write and request this change in the way your interest is paid to you. Interest is always paid without deduction of tax at source on the following holdings:

— 3.5% War Loan

— Government stocks held on the National Savings and Investments Register.

The various rates of tax you can end up paying on your dividend and interest income are set out in Chapter 2. These types of income are treated as the top part of your taxable income. If you have both dividend and savings income, the dividends must always be treated as the highest part. As a result it follows that:

• non-taxpayers will only be able to claim repayment of Income Tax on their savings income where tax at 20% has been deducted at source. The 10% tax credit on UK dividend income is non-repayable;

• individuals liable to Income Tax at only the 10% starting rate will be able to reclaim some of the tax at 20% suffered on their savings income;

• taxpayers who are liable at the basic rate of 22%, but not the top rate, will not face any further tax charge on their dividend and interest income; and

- individuals who are liable to tax at the top rate of 40% will be required to pay Income Tax of a further 20% each year to the extent that their non-dividend savings income takes them above the basic rate band and into the higher tax rate. Where the income beyond the basic rate band comes from UK dividends the extra tax payable is at 32.5%

Derek Bridge receives building society interest, including tax deducted at source, of £1,000 for 2003/04. His earned income, after allowances and reliefs, comes to £8,000. He pays tax for the year as follows:

On the first	£1,960 @ 10%
On the next	£6,040 @ 22%
On his interest income of	£1,000 @ 20%

Davina Wright banks interest and dividend income amounting to £4,300 and £2,800 (gross) respectively during 2003/04. Her earnings, after allowances and reliefs, total £26,500. Her tax charge is worked out as follows:

On the first	£1,960 @ 10%
On the next	£24,540 @ 22%
On her interest income of	£4,000 @ 20%
On her interest income of	£300 @ 40%
On her dividends	£2,800 @ 32.5%

The £4,000 slice of interest income attracts tax at the rate of 20% as it falls within the limit of income of £28,540 taxed at the basic rate.

Many people mistakenly assume – because the dividends and interest mentioned in the top two tables are paid after tax has been deducted – that they do not need to be reported on their annual Tax Return. This misunderstanding is most particularly associated with building society interest. Whatever the totals of your dividends and interest these details must be shown on your Tax Return. The amount of this income may be such as to give rise to a tax charge at the higher rate.

Individuals not liable to tax:

- can arrange to receive their interest gross. This is done by completing special forms which are available at banks, building societies, Post Offices and Tax Offices throughout the country;

- who receive interest from which tax has been deducted, can claim repayment from the Inland Revenue.

Both these measures particularly benefit non-earning married women, pensioners, children and other individuals not liable to Income Tax who choose to invest their savings in accounts with banks and building societies.

Accrued income

Interest on fixed-rate investments is treated as accruing on a day-to-day basis between payment dates. On a sale the vendor is charged to Income Tax on the accrued interest from the previous payment date to the date of the transaction. The purchaser is allowed to deduct this amount from the interest which he receives on the following payment date. These arrangements cover both fixed and variable-rate stocks and bonds, including those issued by governments, companies and local authorities. The arrangements will not affect you if the nominal value of your securities is under £5,000.

The interest on a holding of 8% Treasury Stock 2013 is payable on each 27 March and 27 September. The half-yearly interest on a holding of £20,000, sold for settlement on 10 July 2003, is £1,000.

$$\text{Accrued proportion} = \frac{105}{183} \times £1,000 = £573.77$$

Offshore funds

You may have an investment in an Offshore Fund which distributes substantially all its income by way of dividend. If this is so then the regular dividends you receive are taxed as income and any profit or loss on sale will rank as either a capital gain or loss for the purposes of Capital Gains Tax (see Chapter 12).

Perhaps, however, the Fund pays no dividends and simply accumulates all the income it receives. Then, all the profit on sale is chargeable to Income Tax even if part of the gain could reasonably be considered to represent a capital profit.

Overseas investment income

Generally, income from investments abroad is considered to be income from savings like any other dividends or interest income. Any foreign tax paid can be deducted from the tax payable here on the same dividends or interest. If necessary you must be able to show that you have actually paid, or suffered, the overseas tax.

Non-qualifying life policies

Investment Bonds and Guaranteed Income Bonds offered by most life assurance companies fall within this category. A lump sum premium is paid at the outset. The investor can usually:

- make partial withdrawals from the Bond;

- draw an income; or

- leave it untouched until it is cashed in or forms part of his estate on death.

No tax relief is due on the single premium. The proceeds of a Bond are not liable to Capital Gains Tax or Income Tax at the basic rate. There can be a liability to tax at the difference between the higher and basic rates on chargeable events. These arise on:

- surrender or maturity of the policy;

- on death of the life assured; or

- on withdrawals in excess of the cumulative allowance built up at the time.

At the end of each policy year, an allowance of 5% of the original investment is given. This can be carried forward from year to year. It follows that over a period of 20 years allowances of up to 100% of the initial investment will be given. A taxable gain only arises if the amount of a withdrawal is more than the cumulative allowances at the time. It is the excess which is taxed.

Edward Clark invests £8,000 in an Investment Bond. Withdrawals of £700 and £2,300 are made during the third and sixth policy years. The annual allowance is £400 being 5% of the original investment. A taxable gain of £600 arises in year six as follows:

Number of Policy Years	Cumulative Allowance	Amount Withdrawn	Cumulative Withdrawals	Taxable Amount
	£	£	£	£
1	400	—	—	—
2	800	—	—	—
3	1,200	700	700	—
4	1,600	—	700	—
5	2,000	—	700	—
6	2,400	2,300	3,000	600

When the final chargeable event on a Bond occurs, the taxable gain is calculated by taking into account all previous withdrawals and taxable gains.

The Investment Bond in the illustration above is encashed after nine years for £13,504. The taxable gain amounts to £7,904 as follows:

	£	£
Policy proceeds		13,504
Add: Withdrawals in years 3 and 6		3,000
		16,504
Less: Original investment	8,000	
Amount already taxed	600	
		8,600
Taxable gain on encashment		£7,904

The method of calculating the Income Tax due on the taxable gain involves a number of stages including *top slicing* relief.

Edward Clark, who made a gain of £7,904 on the final encashment of his Investment Bond featured in the two earlier illustrations, is a single man. During 2003/04 his other income, all earnings, amounted to £34,400.

Gain on encashment of Bond	£7,904
Number of years held	9
Taxable slice of gain	£878
Taxable income – excluding slice of gain	
Earnings	34,400
Less: Personal allowance	4,615
	£29,785
Tax applicable to slice of gain	
On first £715 (£30,500 – £29,785) @ 0%	—
On next £163 (excess over £30,500)	
@ 18% (40% – 22%)	£29.34
Average rate on slice	3.34%
The tax payable on the gain =	
£7,904 @ 3.34% =	£264.00

IndividFual Savings Accounts

An Individual Savings Account (ISA) can include three components:

- cash (including National Savings);
- life assurance;
- stocks and shares.

You can subscribe to an ISA if you are:

- both resident and ordinarily resident in the UK for tax purposes; and
- aged 18 or over. 16- and 17-year-olds can invest in the cash component only.

The annual subscription limit is £7,000, of which no more than £3,000 can go into cash and £1,000 into life assurance. Other features of the ISA are:

- The account is completely free of tax.

- There is no statutory lock-in period or minimum subscription. Money can be withdrawn from an ISA whenever you like.

- There is no lifetime investment limit.

- A 10% tax credit is being paid for the first five years of the scheme, that is until 5 April 2004, on dividends from UK equity holdings.

- The scheme is guaranteed to run for at least ten years. It will be reviewed after seven years to decide on any changes after the initial ten-year term.

- Shares acquired under a public offer, or received when a building society or mutual insurer demutualizes, cannot be transferred into an ISA.

The list of qualifying investments allowed for the stocks and shares component of an ISA includes:

- Shares listed on a recognized Stock Exchange.

- Unit trusts.

- Investment trusts.

- Open-ended investment companies.

- Government Stocks with at least five years to go to maturity.

- Share options exercised under an approved SAYE scheme.

- Qualifying Crown Depository Interests.

Each year savers will have two choices when it comes to appointing plan managers. The first option allows them to go to a single manager who must offer an account that can accept the overall subscription. This means that:

- the account must include the stocks and shares component, but does not need to offer either of the other two parts (cash and life assurance);

- savers will be able to subscribe up to £7,000 to the stocks and shares component;

- if, in addition, the manager offers the cash and/or life assurance parts, savers will be able to subscribe up to £3,000 to the cash component and £1,000 to the life assurance part, with the balance going into stocks and shares.

Under the second option savers can go to separate managers – one for each component – and subscribe:

- up to £3,000 in stocks and shares;

- £3,000 to cash; and

- £1,000 to life assurance.

These fixed individual limits will help to ensure that the overall annual investment limit can be satisfactorily monitored.

You will not need to include details of your ISA on your annual Tax Return.

Tax-Exempt Special Savings Accounts

A Tax-Exempt Special Savings Account (TESSA) was a saving scheme with a bank, building society or other institution where the interest was tax free. With the introduction of ISAs no new TESSA could be taken out after 5 April 1999. However, existing TESSAs were allowed to run their course under the following rules:

- The account had to run for the full five years.

- The freedom from Income Tax on the interest was lost if any part of the capital was withdrawn during the five-year investment period.

Any subscriptions after 5 April 1999 did not count towards the investment limits for an ISA. Investors could withdraw interest as it arose during the investment period. Up to the full amount of interest which had been credited to the account could be paid out at any time. However, an amount equivalent to the savings rate of Income Tax on the withdrawal had to be retained within the TESSA. The Income Tax left in the account could be withdrawn in full at the end of the five-year period.

When a TESSA matured, savers could transfer their capital, but not accumulated interest, into the cash component of an ISA. Such a transfer did not affect the amount that could be subscribed to an ISA.

If an investor died during the period when the account was tax free, it came to an end but none of the tax benefits up to that time were lost.

All the paperwork required by the Inland Revenue was handled by the institution with which you had your TESSA. You did not need to mention the tax-free interest on your TESSA in your annual Tax Return.

Personal Equity Plans

Personal Equity Plans (PEPs) are a tax-free way of investing in shares. However, arising from the introduction of ISAs, no new money could be invested in PEPs after 5 April 1999. However, PEPs held at that date can continue under the present rules with the following benefits:

- Any dividends you receive on your UK equity holdings receive a 10% tax credit for five years until 5 April 2004.

- There is no Capital Gains Tax to pay on profits made on selling shares within the plan.

- There are no tax penalties on withdrawing from, or closing down, a plan.

- You do not have to report your PEP dividend income and capital gains to the Inland Revenue on your annual Tax Return.

- The investments that can be held in a PEP are the same as those which are allowed for the stocks and shares component of an ISA.

Friendly Societies

All individuals, including children under 18, can invest up to £270 per annum in a tax-exempt savings plan with a Friendly Society. A family with two children can now save as much as £1,080 per annum through this type of investment.

Enterprise Investment Scheme

The aims of the Scheme are twofold:

- to provide a targeted incentive for equity investment in unquoted trading companies which will help overcome the problems faced by such companies in raising small amounts of equity finance;

- to encourage outside investors, who introduce finance and expertise to a company, by enabling them to take an active part in the management of the company as paid directors without losing entitlement to relief.

The main features of the Scheme are:

- Income Tax relief at 20% on qualifying investments up to £150,000 in any tax year;

- investors are allowed either Income Tax or Capital Gains Tax relief for losses made on the disposal of qualifying shares;

- all shares in a qualifying company must be held for at least three years;

- investors previously unconnected with a qualifying company or its trade can become directors whilst still eligible for relief on their investment;

- relief on up to one-half of the amount that an individual invests between 6 April and 5 October in any tax year can be carried back to the previous tax year, subject to a maximum limit of £25,000.

Venture Capital Trusts

The Venture Capital Trust Scheme is aimed at generating equity investment in dynamic, innovative, unquoted trading companies. The shares of Venture Capital Trusts must be quoted on the Stock Exchange. Individuals who invest in them are eligible for the following Income Tax incentives:

- relief at 20% on subscriptions up to £100,000 in any tax year for new ordinary shares provided the shares are held for at least three years;

- tax-free dividends.

Joint income

Many married couples have bank or building society accounts, Unit Trust holdings or other share investments, or property held in their joint names. They are then treated as if they own the account or asset equally and each will have to pay Income Tax on half the annual income. Alternatively, if capital invested in a Building Society account in joint names actually belongs to husband and wife in unequal shares they can be taxed on their respective shares of the income. The married couple must then declare to the Inland Revenue how the account or other property and the income are shared between them. There is a special form to complete. The declaration applies from the date it is made.

Where one spouse transfers an income-producing asset to the other spouse knowing or expecting that the income will be credited to a joint account on which the donor spouse is free to draw, the income will still be regarded as belonging to the donor spouse for tax purposes.

10 THE FAMILY UNIT

Gone are the days when it was usual for couples to marry. Many people now prefer to live together as partners. Perhaps they may even have children without marrying or marry later on in life.

Living together

There are no special tax breaks for couples living with one another as partners. They are each taxed as single people. Furthermore, it is mandatory that income from jointly owned assets must be split between them in accordance with the ratio of their respective interests in such assets. Assets cannot be transferred between them without avoiding a possible liability to Capital Gains Tax at the time of transfer.

Marriage

Husband and wife:

- are taxed separately on their income and capital gains;

- are each entitled to personal allowances which can be set against their own income, whether from earnings or investments;

- can each have taxable income, after allowances and reliefs of £30,500 for 2003/04 before either of them is liable to tax at the top rate of 40%. They may, of course, need to rearrange their affairs to take maximum advantage of potential tax savings. In contrast to the position of unmarried couples this is easily done;

- must complete their own Tax Returns every year; and

- are each responsible for settling their respective tax liabilities.

Children

A child is:

- treated as an individual for tax purposes like anyone else;
- entitled to the personal allowance, so no tax is probably payable on any earnings from, for example, a daily paper round;
- also a taxable person for the purposes of Capital Gains Tax (Chapter 12) and Inheritance Tax (Chapter 16).

But, the income from a gift by a parent in favour of an unmarried minor child is regarded as the parents' income for tax purposes – subject to an annual £100 limit for small amounts of income. Grandparents or other relatives can, however, give savings to their grandchildren or nieces, nephews, etc., without the same restrictions applying to the taxation of income on any such gifts.

Savers such as children, who are not taxpayers, can elect to receive gross interest on their bank or building society accounts. As an alternative to this type of investment for your child's savings, why not take a look at the Children's Bonus Bonds issued by National Savings and Investments which are particularly suitable for gifts from parents. The return on these Bonds is exempt from both Income Tax and Capital Gains Tax.

There is no general tax allowance for children. However:

- you should be able to claim Child Benefit and may be due the new Child Tax Credit (see Chapter 2);
- depending on your personal circumstances you may be entitled to one or more of the numerous other Social Security benefits associated with children.

It is down to parents or guardians to complete and sign Tax Returns or Repayment Claims for their children up to age 18.

The Child Trust Fund

As announced by the Chancellor in his 2003 Budget the Child Trust Fund (CTF) will be introduced in 2005.

Under the proposals for the CTF:

- Children born from 1 September 2002 will be provided with an endowment of £250 at birth.

- Children from low-income families will receive an additional £250.

- The Government will make a further payment, the amount of which is still to be decided, when children reach age 7.

- Up to £1,200 can be added to the Fund each year by family and friends.

CTF accounts are expected to become available in April 2005. Vouchers and information are being sent to parents of children born between September 2002 and April 2005. The vouchers will have a higher value recognizing that there will be less time for the CTF accounts of children born in this period to grow in value.

The Fund will help build up a stock of assets for each young person to reinvest or access when they reach 18 years of age. All income and capital growth will be tax free.

Separation and divorce

Not only does the breakdown of a marriage cause much personal suffering but it invariably has consequences for tax purposes.

A married couple are no longer considered to be living together when:

- they are separated by a Deed or Court Order; or

- they are living apart in such a way that permanent separation is inevitable.

If a married couple are entitled to the married couple's allowance, the full allowance can be claimed by the husband for the tax year in which the marriage fails, but if he remarries in the same year he cannot also claim that part of the allowance due for the period following the wedding.

Maintenance payments are tax free in the hands of the recipient, but only limited tax relief is available to the payer of maintenance under a Court Order, Child Support Agency assessment or written agreement as follows:

- either the payer or recipient must be born before 6 April 1935;

- the payment must be to the divorced or separated spouse;

- the maximum amount of tax relief to which the payer is entitled is 10% of the lesser of £2,150 or the actual maintenance paid each year;

- no tax relief can be claimed on maintenance paid to, or for the benefit of, children of the marriage.

Old age

When it comes to tax, getting older does not mean an easier life. Pensioners have to deal with the tax system in the same way as everyone else. Nevertheless, there are some factors which are only relevant to:

- the finances of elderly persons; and

- working out how much tax they must pay each year.

First and foremost come the age allowances. In Chapter 2 I explained how a pensioner calculates the amount of these allowances to which he or she is entitled.

Men qualify to receive the State Pension when they reach age 65; for women it is currently age 60. The State Pension includes:

- the basic retirement (or old person's) pension;

- a state earnings-related pension (SERPS/S2P);

- a graduated pension;

- the age addition if you are over 80.

All pensions, including a State Pension, are taxable. There is, however, no mechanism to deduct any income tax at source from payment of the State Pension. Therefore, in addition to including a pensioner's personal allowance in the coding notice of an occupational or personal pension taxed under PAYE, it also incorporates a deduction from allowances equivalent to the annual amount of the State Pension. In this way:

- the tax due on the State Pension is collected; and

- the need to make a direct tax payment is avoided.

The significance of the following letters at the end of a Code Number is as follows:

- V – indicates the pensioner is entitled to both the personal and married couple's allowances for ages 65–74 and pays tax at the basic rate;

- P – indicates the full personal allowance is due for those aged 65–74;

- Y – means you are due the full personal allowance for age 75 and over; and

- T – applies in most other circumstances.

If a pensioner's State Pension exceeds his or her personal allowance, the Inland Revenue issue a 'K' Coding. The amount of the negative allowance is then added to the pension on which tax is paid.

Taxpayers approaching State Pension age should make sure that their Notice of Coding is changed to include an estimate of the amount of their State Pension for the year. Usually the Inland Revenue sends such taxpayers a Form P161 asking for details about pension entitlement. This information is then used to amend tax codes as appropriate.

Nowadays many people carry on working after they retire from their main job or self-employment. They may decide to make use of all the knowledge and experience built up during their working lives by setting up in business as a consultant, or take a part-time position in, for example, a retail outlet.

Owen Wilcox is single and 68. During 2003/04 he received a State Pension of £86.15 per week and an annual pension from his previous employer of £6,000. To keep himself occupied he worked part-time at his local DIY Store earning a weekly wage of £105 for 46 weeks of the year. Owen paid income tax for 2003/04 of £1,681.00 as follows:

	Income	Tax
	£	£
State Pension	4,480	
Occupational Pension	6,000	618.40
Wages	4,830	1,062.60
	15,310	£1,681.00
Less: Personal Allowance	6,600	
Taxable Income	£8,710	

Income Tax payable	
£1,960 @ 10%	196.00
£6,750 @ 22%	1,485.00
	£1,681.00

The tax code used for working out the income tax to be deducted from Owen's occupational pension is 212P. This is based on the difference between Owen's personal age allowance of £6,600 and his State Pension of £4,480. Tax at the basic rate of 22%, under a BR Code, would have been deducted from Owen's wage from the DIY store.

To gain maximum advantage from the personal age and married couple's allowance, as well as paying tax at the 10% rate on the full amount of income in the starting rate band – £1,960 for 2003/04 – elderly married couples with modest incomes may need to transfer capital between themselves.

Bert and Mavis Wilkins, a married couple, both in their late 60s, whose joint income for 2003/04 amounted to £37,000, paid Income Tax of £4,874.50 on this sum. This mainly related to Bert's income as follows:

	Bert	Mavis
	£	£
State Pensions	4,027	2,410
Occupational Pensions	10,973	2,500
Building Society Interest		
Gross equivalent	10,000	890
Interest on British Government Stocks	5,000	1,200
	30,000	7,000
Less: Personal Allowance	4,615	6,600
Taxable Income	£25,385	£400
Income Tax Payable		
£1,960/£400 @ 10%	196.00	40.00
£8,425 @ 22%	1,853.50	—
£15,000 @ 20% (savings income)	3,000.00	—
	5,049.50	40.00

Less: Relief for married couple's allowance – £2,150 @ 10%	215.00	—
	£4,834.50	£40.00

Bert's income is above the upper limit for entitlement to personal age or married couple's allowances, whereas Mavis has insufficient income to benefit from the full starting-rate tax band of £1,960.

Significant tax savings of £890.20 for 2003/04 could have been achieved by the couple if Bert had transferred capital to Mavis as follows:

	Bert	Mavis
	£	£
State Pensions	4,027	2,410
Occupational Pensions	10,973	2,500
Building Society Interest Gross equivalent	2,000	8,890
Interest on British Government Stocks	1,700	4,500
	18,700	18,300
Less: Personal Allowance	6,400	6,600
Taxable Income	£12,300	£11,700
Income Tax payable		
£1960 @ 10%	196.00	196.00
£6,640 @ 22%	1,460.80	—
£3,700/£9,740 @ 20% (savings income)	740.00	1,948.00
	2,396.80	2,144.00
Less: Relief for married couple's allowance - £5,565 @ 10%	556.50	—
	£1,840.30	£2,144.00

Death

Sadly, death comes to all of us and has consequences for taxation which are:

- the married couple's allowance is not restricted in the year of death of either spouse;

- where the husband dies first, he is due his full personal allowance in the year of death. If he cannot use up the full married couple's allowance, because he has a low income, then the balance can be transferred to his widow;

- if the wife dies before her husband she will be due her full personal allowance in the year of death.

11 THE OVERSEAS ELEMENT

Apart from some special cases, the amount of tax you pay each year depends on whether you are resident in the United Kingdom (UK) and, to a lesser extent, on your domicile status. If you live permanently in the UK then, generally, all your income arising in this country will be liable to UK taxation. Overseas income is similarly taxable although special rules apply in taxing foreign income of individuals resident, but not domiciled, in the UK.

Not only are the two concepts of domicile and residence of fundamental importance in determining the extent of an individual's liability to UK taxation on income, they are of equal significance for the purposes of both Capital Gains Tax and Inheritance Tax.

Domicile

Your domicile will generally be considered to be the country or state which you regard as your permanent homeland. Your domicile is separate from your residence or nationality. When you are born you acquire a domicile of origin from your father. You can abandon your original domicile by birth if you settle in another country or state with a view to making it your new permanent home. Provided you sever all links with your current country of domicile you can move towards acquiring a domicile of choice in the new country. You should be prepared to provide a substantial amount of evidence that you propose to live there for ever.

A wife's domicile is not necessarily the same as her husband's domicile if they were married at some time after the end of 1973. It is decided by the same factors as for any other individual who is able to have an independent domicile. A woman who married before the beginning of 1974 automatically acquired the domicile of her husband on marriage. So long as the marriage lasts, her domicile only alters when there is any change in the domicile of her husband.

If you think you have good grounds for believing that you should not be regarded as domiciled in the UK you should write to your tax office about this. Usually, you can then expect to receive a questionnaire which you should fill in and send back to your tax office. The information you have supplied will be considered by the Inland Revenue Specialist Department that deals with these matters. In due course you will receive a ruling on your domicile status.

Residence and ordinary residence

There is no statutory definition of residence and ordinary residence. Each case must be judged on the facts. What follows is a summary of the main factors that will be taken into account.

Without exception you will always be regarded as resident in the UK if you spend 183 days or more here in the tax year. Days of arrival in, and departure from, the UK are normally left out of account in working out the number of days spent here.

If you are here for less than 183 days you will still be treated as resident where you visit the UK regularly and after four tax years your visits during those years average 91 days or more in a tax year. From the fifth year you are treated as a UK resident.

You are also regarded as ordinarily resident in the UK if you are resident here from year to year. It is possible to be resident, but not ordinarily resident. For example, you may normally live outside the UK but are in this country for at least 183 days in a tax year. Conversely you can occasionally be considered to be ordinarily resident, but not actually resident, for a particular tax year. This could happen if you live in the UK but, for some reason, are abroad for a complete tax year.

Calculating annual average visits

The set formula to be used in working out the average number of days spent in the UK each year is:

$$\frac{\text{total visits to the UK (in days)}}{\text{total period since leaving (in days)}} \times 365 \text{ days} = \text{annual average visits}$$

The maximum period over which the average is taken is four years.

Thomas Winter, a retired solicitor, left the UK on 23 November 2000. In the period from the date of his departure to 5 April 2001 he visited the UK for 43 days. In the following three tax years to 5 April 2004, he spent 110, 85 and 57 days in the UK. The average number of days in the UK works out at 87.61 as follows:

$$\frac{43 + 110 + 85 + 57}{133 + 365 + 366 + 365} = \frac{295}{1,229} \times 365 = 87.61 \text{ days}$$

As this is less than the 91 days per annum average Thomas will be treated as non-resident throughout the period.

Working abroad – long absences

Poor job prospects in the UK, together with higher salaries and low taxation abroad, may prompt you to look for work overseas. This is likely to involve living abroad permanently for a time. Your probable residence status is clearly set out in paragraphs 2:2 and 2:3 of the Inland Revenue booklet IR20 – *Residents and Non-Residents* – as follows:

'If you leave the UK to work full time abroad under a contract of employment, you are treated as not resident and not ordinarily resident if you meet all the following conditions:

- your absence from the UK and your employment abroad both last for at least a whole tax year;
- during your absence any visits you make to the UK
  - total less than 183 days in any tax year, and
  - average less than 91 days a tax year (the average is taken over the period of absence up to a maximum of four years; any dates spent in the UK because of exceptional circumstances beyond your control, for example the illness of yourself or a member of your immediate family, are not normally counted for this purpose).

Should you meet all of the above conditions you are treated as not resident and not ordinarily resident in the UK from the day after you leave the UK to the date before you return to the UK at the end of your employment abroad. You are treated as coming to the UK permanently on the day you return from your employment abroad and as resident and ordinarily resident from that date.'

There will be no tax to pay here on your salary for the part of the tax year after you have left the UK.

There is no specific definition of when employment abroad is 'full time'. Each particular case must be considered on all the facts. Nevertheless, where your employment involves a standard pattern of hours, it will be regarded as full time if your working hours each week are comparable with those that would be worked in the UK. Furthermore, several part-time jobs all at the same time could be taken as constituting full-time employment.

If you leave the UK to work full time in a trade, profession or vocation overseas and fulfil the same conditions as anyone taking up full-time employment abroad then your UK residence status will be determined in the same way.

You may well take your spouse with you. By concession he or she may also be regarded as neither resident nor ordinarily resident for the same period even if your spouse does not work abroad.

Working abroad – expenses

Tax relief is allowed on travel expenses you incur in relation to your overseas employment. Nor will you be taxed on the cost of board and lodging provided for you where the expenses are borne by your employer.

Generally, whenever your job takes you overseas, even for short periods, you will not be taxed on the cost of your travelling expenses so long as your employer meets the bills. This also applies to the costs of unlimited return visits to the UK during longer assignments abroad.

No taxable benefit arises where your employer meets the travelling costs of your spouse and children to visit you overseas. Not more than two return visits by the same person are allowed each year, and you must be working abroad for a continuous period of at least 60 days.

Leaving the UK permanently

Where you go abroad to live permanently, or to live outside the UK for three years or more, you will provisionally be considered neither resident nor ordinarily resident in the UK from the day following your departure. You should be prepared to provide sufficient evidence of your intention to make a permanent home somewhere outside the UK. Provided you do not infringe the rules about visits to the UK the provisional non-resident ruling will subsequently be confirmed by the Inland Revenue. You are entitled to full allowances and reliefs for the year of departure.

Before you leave, ask your tax office for the special form (P85) to be completed by individuals going abroad. The information in the form about your intended residence position will enable the Inland Revenue to make an in-year tax refund to you if, for example, you are claiming split-year treatment.

When you become not ordinarily resident in the UK you can apply to receive interest on any bank or building society account here without deduction of tax. Similarly, Income Tax is not charged on the interest from certain UK Government securities.

Allowances for non-UK residents

You may be able to claim UK tax allowances if you are not resident here. If you are eligible to claim you will generally be entitled to the same allowances as an individual resident in the UK. The following individuals can claim:

- a citizen of the Commonwealth;
- a citizen of a state within the European Union;
- a present or former employee of the British Crown;
- a resident of the Isle of Man or the Channel Islands;
- certain other specific classes of individuals.

Income from UK property

Many individuals choose to rent out their homes while they are away, particularly when they go to work abroad. You can apply to the Inland Revenue for a certificate authorizing your tenant, or managing agent, to make payments of rent to you without deducting UK tax. If no such certificate is issued, tax at the basic rate must be withheld from all remittances of rent to you.

Even though you are not resident in the UK you could still be liable to UK tax on income arising from the letting out of UK property.

This is so, whether or not tax is deducted by your tenant or letting agent. However, you will not actually have any UK tax to pay if your total income, including your income from property after allowable expenses, chargeable to UK tax is less than any allowances which you may be entitled to claim.

Double taxation relief

If you move to a country with which the UK has concluded a Double Taxation Agreement, you may be able to claim partial or full exemption from UK tax on certain types of income from UK sources. Normally, you should be entitled to some measure of relief from UK tax on pensions and annuities, royalties and dividends. Many Double Taxation Agreements contain clauses dealing with the special circumstances of teachers and researchers, students and apprentices, and entertainers and sportsmen/women.

Going abroad – Capital Gains Tax

If you have been resident in the UK for at least four out of the last seven years ending with the day you leave and, within five years, you return here to take up residence for tax purposes again, then the concessionary split-year tax treatment does not apply for the purposes of Capital Gains Tax. You will be classified as a UK resident for the entire tax years of both departure and return.

It follows that gains realized in the tax year of departure will be taxed in that year. All gains in subsequent years, including the year of return, will be subject to Capital Gains Tax in the year when residence resumes. Profits made on assets bought and sold during the years of non-UK tax residence will not, however, be liable to Capital Gains Tax in the UK.

Taking up UK residence

Perhaps you have been working overseas, your contract has come to an end and you are thinking about returning here. Before you take up UK residence again there are some specific tax-planning points which must be considered. For example, any bank deposit or building society accounts should be closed before you return as you could otherwise face the prospect of a charge to UK Income Tax on interest accrued, but not credited, during your period of non-residence.

If the UK is not your normal homeland you should initially be able to satisfy our Inland Revenue Authorities that you have an overseas domicile. Any income from investments here is taxable as it arises. Your overseas investment income is not taxed unless it is actually remitted or enjoyed here. Where your job is with either a UK or an overseas employer, and the duties of your employment are performed wholly in the UK, the full amount of your salary is taxable here. Appendix 8 at the end of the book is a summary of the scope of liability to Income Tax of earnings.

You will be treated as resident and ordinarily resident from the date you arrive if you are either coming here permanently or intending to stay for at least three years. You will be able to claim full UK personal allowances for the year of arrival.

You should let the Inland Revenue know when you come to the UK. You will normally be asked to complete a Form P86 which will help to determine your residence status. The form also includes a section on domicile so that it will be possible, in straightforward cases, to deal with both your residence status and domicile together. This will apply, for example, if you:

- have never been domiciled within the UK;

- have come here only to work; and

- intend to leave the UK once your employment ceases.

In less straightforward cases where domicile affects liability to UK taxation, you will need to obtain another form in order to give the further information necessary to determine your domicile.

12 CAPITAL GAINS TAX

As its name implies, Capital Gains Tax is a tax on profits you realize from the disposal of capital assets. As with most other forms of taxation there is the usual list of exceptions to this general rule. Gambling, pools or lottery winnings, personal or professional damages and mortgage cashbacks are not taxable. Neither are gains realized on disposing of any of the assets in the following table:

- private cars

- National Savings

- your private residence

- chattels, with an expected life of more than 50 years, sold for less than £6,000

- British Government securities and many corporate bonds

- shares issued under the Business Expansion Scheme after 18 March 1986 on their first disposal

- shares issued under the Enterprise Investment Scheme on their first disposal, so long as the tax relief has not been withdrawn

- shares in Venture Capital Trusts

- investments in a Personal Equity Plan

- investments in an Individual Savings Account

- life assurance policies – unless purchased by you

- charitable gifts

- gifts for the public benefit

- foreign currency for personal expenditure.

The list of taxable gains includes profits made from disposing of property, shareholdings, unit trust holdings, works of art and foreign currency for other than personal expenditure.

Rate of tax

For the 2003/04 tax year the first £7,900 of chargeable gains you realize are tax free. Gains in excess of the annual tax-free allowance are charged at your Income Tax rates found by adding the gains to your taxable income.

Isaac Woolf realized gains of £18,000 during 2003/04. His taxable income, after personal allowances and reliefs, was £24,000. The Capital Gains Tax he owes for the year is £2,740 as follows:

	£
Realized gains	18,000
Less: Exemption limit	7,900
	£10,100
Tax payable	
£6,500 @ 20% (Savings Rate)	1,300
£3,600 @ 40%	1,440
2003/04 Capital Gains Tax payable	£2,740

The amount of Capital Gains Tax at 20% is worked out on the difference between the £30,500 limit of income taxable at the starting and basic rates and Isaac's income of £24,000.

Any allowances or reliefs that you are unable to use because your income is too low cannot be set against your capital gains.

Married couples

Husband and wife are:

- Each entitled to the annual exemption limit.

- Taxed separately on the chargeable gains they realize in the tax year above the annual exemption limit.

A married couple living together can transfer assets between them free of tax. Assets are regarded as passing from one spouse to the other without either gain or loss. For tax purposes the recipient is deemed to have acquired such assets at the other spouse's cost. The exemption from taxing gains on transfers between spouses ceases when a couple permanently separates.

In cases where a married couple hold an asset in their joint names, any gain is apportioned between them in the ratio of their respective interests in the asset at the time of disposal. This treatment may not necessarily follow the split of the income for income tax purposes. Here the law generally assumes a married couple are equally entitled to the income even if, in fact, this is not so. Where a couple have jointly made a declaration to the Inland Revenue of the ratio in which an asset and the income derived from it are shared between them, the same split will follow for Capital Gains Tax purposes.

Losses

Losses can be set against gains made in the same tax year. Unused losses can be carried forward to be set against gains in subsequent tax years without time limit. They then reduce the amount of your gains in excess of the annual exemption limit.

Sally Rogers had capital losses of £5,200 available for carry-forward at 5 April 2003. During 2003/04 she realized gains of £9,800 and made losses of £900.

Her capital gains position for the year is:

	£	£
Gains realized in the year		9,800
Less: Losses in the year	900	
brought forward (part)	1,000	
		1,900
2003/04 Exemption limit		£7,900

The unused losses of £4,000 can be carried forward to be set against gains in later years.

Losses realized by one spouse cannot be set against gains realized by the other spouse. This restriction on the set-off of losses also extends to unused losses at 5 April 1990.

A loss:

- arising on the sale or gift of an investment to a person connected with the individual making the disposal can only be set off against a gain from a similar disposal at a later date;

- can be claimed where the value of an asset you own becomes negligible or nil. You do not actually have to dispose of the asset. The loss arises on the date that the relief is claimed. In practice, however, a two-year period is allowed from the end of the tax year in which the asset became of negligible value;

- on shares you subscribe for in a trading company not quoted on a recognized Stock Exchange can be set against your income, rather than against other capital gains. This applies whether you realize a loss on disposing of such shares, or they become worthless.

The computation of gains

The taxable gain on the disposal of an asset is calculated by making various deductions from the sale proceeds, as follows:

- the cost of acquisition, and

- the incidental costs of buying and selling the asset, such as legal fees, valuation expenses, stamp duty, and

- any additional expenditure incurred on enhancing the value of the asset during the period of ownership, and

- the indexation allowance.

There are occasions when a different figure from the actual disposal proceeds is substituted in the calculation. For example, this happens when you make a gift or sell an asset at a nominal value to a close member of your family. You must then bring into the computation of the capital gain the open-market value of the asset at the time of disposal.

The date of sale of an asset is taken as the date when the contract for sale is made. The same rule determines the date of acquisition.

Later on in this chapter I shall deal with the special rules in cases where you dispose of assets you owned on either 31 March 1982 or 6 April 1965.

The indexation allowance

This allowance, which has now been frozen, measures the impact of inflation on both the cost of an asset and any other expenditure you have incurred on enhancing its value. The rules dealing with the calculation of the allowance are:

- the allowance is governed by the movement in the Retail Prices Index in the period of ownership up to April 1998. For assets that you have owned since before April 1982 the starting date for calculating the indexation allowance is March 1982;

- when you dispose of an asset that you acquired before 6 April 1982 the indexation allowance can be calculated on either the market value of the asset at 31 March 1982 or its actual cost, whichever is greater. Where you elect for the capital gains on all disposals of assets that you owned on 31 March 1982 to be worked out on their values at that date, ignoring original costs, the indexation allowance can only be calculated on those values;

- the allowance will not be given where an asset is sold at a loss. Neither can the indexation allowance turn a gain into a loss. It can only serve to reduce a gain to nil.

No indexation allowance is allowed in working out the chargeable gain on assets that are acquired on or after 1 April 1998. For disposals of assets acquired previously the indexation allowance is given for periods up to April 1998, but not thereafter.

Appendix 9 at the end of the book sets out the indexation allowance for April 1998. It is not possible in the space permitted to reproduce previous indexation allowance tables. If you need this information you should approach the tax office responsible for your tax affairs.

A freehold property was purchased in November 1987 for £40,000. The legal fees and stamp duty on the purchase came to £1,340. An extension was added in February 1990 at a cost of £9,400.

Contracts for sale were exchanged in November 2003. It was sold for

£96,000. The estate agents' commission, including the costs of advertising, and solicitors' fees, came to £2,820.

The indexation allowance between November 1987 and April 1998 is 0.573, and from February 1990 to April 1998 is 0.353.

The chargeable gain, before taper relief, is £15,435 as follows:

		£	£
Sale price			96,000
Less: Costs of sale			2,820
			93,180
Less: Acquisition price	40,000		
Costs of purchase	1,340		
Enhancement expenditure			
– extension	9,400		
	50,740		
Indexation allowance:			
£41,340 x 0.573	23,687		
£9,400 x 0.353	3,318		77,745
Chargeable gain, before taper relief			£15,435

Taper relief

Chargeable gains are subject to taper relief, the replacement for the indexation allowance. The main features of taper relief are:

- The proportion of a chargeable gain brought in to charge to tax is reduced by reference to the number of whole years (up to a maximum of ten) that an asset has been held.

- For this purpose a year is any continuous period of 12 months.

- Fractions of a year are ignored.

- There are two different percentage tables, one for business assets and one for non-business assets. The reductions for business assets are far more generous than those for non-business assets.

Gains on business assets		Gains on non-business assets	
Number of whole years in qualifying holding period	*Percentage of gain chargeable*	*Number of whole years in qualifying holding period*	*Percentage of gain chargeable*
1	50	1	100
2	25	2	100
3	25	3	95
4	25	4	90
5	25	5	85
6	25	6	80
7	25	7	75
8	25	8	70
9	25	9	65
10 or more	25	10 or more	60

For the purpose of these rules the qualifying holding period for an asset is the time between:

- The later of the date of acquisition and 6 April 1998, and

- The date of disposal.

The qualifying holding period is increased by one year for a non-business asset that was acquired before 17 March 1998.

Allowable losses are not tapered. They are set off against chargeable gains before taper relief. The treatment is similar for both losses made in the same tax year as well as those brought forward from earlier years. By deducting losses from gains, before applying the taper, means that both losses and gains are effectively subjected to taper relief. Nevertheless, you can set losses against gains for this purpose in order to achieve the lowest possible tax charge. This means setting them:

- first against any gains on which no taper relief is available;

- then against any gains where the taper relief is less than on other gains, and so on.

While indexation was deducted in working out the amount of a gain, taper relief is given after the chargeable gain has been calculated. Thus, in a case where a chargeable gain arises on a disposal to which both frozen indexation allowance and taper relief apply:

- The indexation allowance is first of all taken off to arrive at the amount of gain;

- Any allowable losses are deducted from the gain;

- Finally, taper relief is based on the net amount of the gain.

Andrew Walton bought shares in a quoted company, for which he does not work, in April 1993 for £5,100. He sold the shares in February 2004 for £18,900. In 2003/04 Andrew also realized a loss of £2,600 on the disposal of another asset.

The indexation allowance between April 1993 and April 1998 is 0.156.

Andrew's net chargeable gain for 2003/04 is £8,324 as follows:

		£	£
Sale proceeds of shares			18,900
Less: Cost price	5,100		
Indexation allowance 0.156	795		
			5,895
			13,005
Less: Loss on sale of other asset			2,600
			10,405
Less: Taper relief – 20%			2,081
Net chargeable gain			£8,324

Andrew owned the shares for five complete tax years after 5 April 1998. As he bought the shares before 17 March 1998, Andrew benefits from a bonus year and is entitled to six years of non-business assets taper relief.

Business assets

As the table on page 130 illustrates, the rate of Taper Relief applied to gains on disposals of business assets is far more generous than the corresponding reduction for non-business assets.

The following list of assets are those which qualify for the enhanced rate of taper relief applicable to business assets:

- *Assets used in your trade or by a company in which you have a qualifying shareholding.

- *Any of your assets used in your job where you work for a trading employer.

- *All shareholdings held by employees and others in unquoted trading companies.

- *All shareholdings held by employees in quoted trading companies.

- *Shareholdings in a quoted trading company where the holder is not an employee but can exercise at least 5% of the voting rights.

- Shares owned by employees and office holders of a non-trading company provided the employee does not have a material interest in the company. This is defined as a right to more than 10% of:

    — the profit;

    — the assets on winding up;

    — the voting rights;

    — any class of share capital.

* The qualifying criteria under these headings were relaxed from 6 April 2000.

Where an asset only satisfies the definition of business assets from 6 April 2000 it will be regarded as a non-business asset up to that date. Accordingly the gain will have to be time apportioned so that part will come within the rules for business assets taper relief with the balance as a non-business asset.

Patricia Dunne acquired a shareholding in her employer's quoted company in September 1995 for £3,200. Her stake in the company is tiny. She sells the shares in June 2003 realizing £14,500.

The indexation allowance between September 1995 and April 1998 is 0.08.

Until 5 April 2000 the shares were not business assets for taper relief purposes. They did so qualify from 6 April 2000 up to the date of sale. The gain must be apportioned throughout the period of ownership from 6 April 1998.

Patricia's total net chargeable gain for 2003/04 is £5,113 as follows:

	£	£
Sale proceeds of shares		14,500
Less: Cost price	3,200	
Indexation allowance 0.08	256	
		3,456
Gain before taper relief		£11,044

(a) Period as non-business asset

April 1998 to April 2000   24 months

$$\frac{\text{April 1998 to April 2000}}{\text{April 1998 to June 2003}} = \frac{24 \text{ months}}{62 \text{ months}} \times £11,044 = \quad 4,275$$

Less: Taper relief – 20%
(five years plus the bonus year)   855

Chargeable gain   £3,420

(b) Period as business asset

April 2000 to June 2003   38 months

$$\frac{\text{April 2000 to June 2003}}{\text{April 1998 to June 2003}} = \frac{38 \text{ months}}{62 \text{ months}} \times £11,044 = \quad 6,769$$

Less: Taper relief – 75% (five years plus the bonus year)   5,076

Chargeable gain   £1,693

Assets owned on 31 March 1982

Gains and losses on disposals of assets that you owned on 31 March 1982 can be calculated solely by reference to their market value at that date, ignoring original costs. In most cases, these rules will mean your capital gains are reduced compared with the calculation based on historical cost only.

A freehold property purchased in 1976 for £20,000 was sold in October 2003 for £84,000. At 31 March 1982 it was valued at £38,000. The indexation allowance between March 1982 and April 1998 is 1.047.

The chargeable gain is £4,972 as follows:

	On 31 March 1982 Value		On Historical Cost	
	£	£	£	£
Sale price		84,000		84,000
Less: March 1982 value	38,000		—	
Acquisition cost	—		20,000	
Indexation allowance				
£38,000 x 1.047	39,786		39,786	
		77,786		59,786
		£6,214		£24,214
Lesser gain			6,214	
Less: Taper relief – 20%			1,242	
2003/04 chargeable gain			£4,972	

Needless to say, there are special rules where the calculations based firstly on the March 1982 value and secondly on historical cost give different results, as follows:

On March 1982 Value	On Historical Cost	Chargeable Gain/Loss
Gain of £3,810	Gain of £2,150	£2,150 Gain
Loss of £515	Loss of £95	£95 Loss
Loss of £490	Gain of £760	neither gain nor loss
Gain of £2,435	Loss of £1,640	neither gain nor loss

You can, however, elect for the capital gains on all disposals of assets which you owned on 31 March 1982 to be worked out by reference to their values at that date, ignoring original costs. Once made, the election cannot be revoked.

Quoted stocks and shares

Prior to 6 April 1982 each shareholding was regarded as a single asset. This was commonly known as a 'pool'. Each additional purchase of the same class of shares or a sale of part of the holding represented either an addition to, or a disposal out of, the pool. With the introduction of the indexation allowance this changed. Each shareholding acquired after 5 April 1982 represented a separate asset. A subsequent addition to a holding you owned at 5 April 1982 could not be added to the pool.

The rules were altered from 6 April 1985. Shares of the same class were again regarded as a single asset growing or diminishing on each acquisition or disposal. This form of 'pooling' applied to shares acquired after 5 April 1982 unless they had already been disposed of before 6 April 1985; it is called a 'new holding'. A pool which was frozen under the 1982 rules stays that way. It remains a single asset which cannot grow by subsequent acquisitions and is known as a '1982 holding'.

A '1982 holding' is treated like any other asset in calculating the indexation allowance. This is not so for a 'new holding'. It had to be kept continually indexed each time there was an addition to, or a disposal out of, the pool up until April 1998.

The introduction of taper relief means that 'pooling' ceases for acquisitions of shares on or after 6 April 1998. This is necessary since the date of each acquisition needs to be recorded and retained.

The procedure for matching shares sold with their corresponding acquisition is as follows:

- shares acquired on the same day;

- shares acquired within 30 days following a disposal;

- shares acquired before the disposal, but after 5 April 1998, identifying the most recent acquisitions first;

- shares comprised in a 'new holding', the 1982–1998 share pool;

- shares within a '1982 holding', the 1965–1982 share pool;

- any shares acquired before 6 April 1965, last in first out;

- shares acquired more than 30 days after the disposal.

Lauren Dawson bought 2,000 shares in a quoted company on 9 September 1995 at a total cost of £2,200. She sold the entire holding on 27 November 2003 for £3,400. She then went on to reacquire the same number of shares in the company on 6 December 2003 for £3,150.

As the repurchase took place within 30 days of the sale the profit on the disposal is:

	£
Sale of 2,000 shares on 27 November 2003	3,400
Less: Cost of reacquisition on 6 December 2003	3,150
Chargeable gain	£250

Gareth Davies made the following purchases in the shares of a quoted company:

Date	Number of Shares	Cost
May 1974	1,500	£1,875
Jan 1981	2,500	£3,500
Mar 1985	3,000	£3,900
Feb 1988	1,000	£1,700
June 1998	2,000	£5,600

In March 2004 he sold 9,000 shares for £32,400. The shares were valued at £1.50 each on 31 March 1982. The indexation allowance is:

1.047 between March 1982 and April 1998

0.117 between March 1985 and February 1988

0.568 between February 1988 and April 1998

2,000 shares sold must first of all be identified with the acquisition after 5 April 1998 as follows:

	£
Cost of 2,000 shares in June 1998	5,600
Proceeds of sale of 2,000 shares	7,200
	1,600

Less: Taper relief – 15%	240
Chargeable gain	1,360

Secondly, 4,000 shares sold must be identified with those in the 'new holding' as follows:

	£
Cost of 3,000 shares in March 1985	3,900
Indexation allowance to February 1988 – 0.117	456
	4,356
Cost of 1,000 shares in February 1988	1,700
	6,056
Indexation allowance to April 1998 – 0.568	3,439
	9,495
Proceeds of sale of 4,000 shares	14,400
	4,905
Less: Taper relief – 20%	981
Chargeable gain	£3,924

The remaining 3,000 shares sold are then identified with part of the shares acquired before 31 March 1982. As the average cost is £1.34 per share it is beneficial to base the capital gain on the share price at 31 March 1982 as follows:

	£
Value of 3,000 shares at March 1982	4,500
Indexation allowance to April 1998 – 1.047	4,711
	9,211
Proceeds of sale of 3,000 shares	10,800
	1,589
Less: Taper relief – 20%	318
Chargeable gain	£1,271

The total chargeable gain on the sale is £6,555.

Whenever you receive a bonus issue of shares of the same class as an existing holding the date of their acquisition is the same as that of the original holding. The same principle applies to further shares acquired under a rights issue.

Where a company in which you have a holding is taken over and you receive:

- shares in the new company in exchange for your shares in the company taken over, no disposal takes place at that time. Your new holding is regarded as having been acquired at the same time, and for the same price, as the old one;

- a mixture of cash and shares in the new company, a gain or loss arises on the cash element of the take-over. It is then necessary to apportion the cost price of the old shares, including any indexation allowance up to the date of the take-over, between the cash received and the value of the shareholding in the new company at the time.

Unquoted investments

Many of the rules dealing with quoted stocks and shares also apply to computations on disposals of unquoted investments. For example, the indexing rules apply in the same way as they do to quoted shares.

Most of the special rules dealing with unquoted investments apply to assets held at 6 April 1965 when Capital Gains Tax was introduced.

Assets held on 6 April 1965

Following the introduction of rules dealing with assets owned on 31 March 1982, the special rules for assets held on 6 April 1965 are likely to be of less significance.

The method of computation:

- is known as 'time-apportionment';

- does not apply to quoted stocks and shares, only to unquoted investments and other assets such as land;

- is designed to eliminate from the charge to tax the profit on sale attributable to the period up to 5 April 1965;

- achieves this result by assuming that the asset increased in value at a standard rate throughout the period of ownership.

It is the gain, net of indexaton, that is time-apportioned. For assets acquired before 6 April 1945 time-apportionment benefit is limited to 20 years.

Instead of relying on the time-apportionment method, a taxpayer can make an irrevocable election for the value of the asset on 6 April 1965 to be substituted in a calculation of the capital gain arising on sale.

A property purchased in June 1959 for £5,000 was sold in late April 2003 for £45,000. An election for the 6 April 1965 value is not beneficial. At 31 March 1982 it was worth £20,000. The indexation allowance between March 1982 and April 1998 is 1.047.

The first calculation of the chargeable gain is:

	£
Sale proceeds	45,000
Less: Purchase price	5,000
Gross gain	40,000
Less: Indexation allowance £20,000 x 1.047	20,940
Indexed gain	£19,060

Time-apportionment:

$$\frac{\text{April 1965 to April 2003}}{\text{June 1959 to April 2003}} = \frac{456 \text{ months}}{526 \text{ months}} \times £19,060 = \quad 16,523$$

The second calculation of the chargeable gain is:

	£	£
Sale proceeds		45,000
Less: 31 March 1982 value	20,000	
Indexation allowance		
£20,000 x 1.047	20,940	
		40,940
		£4,060

It is advantageous for the 31 March 1982 value to be used in calculating the chargeable gain, which is £4,060, subject to taper relief.

For quoted shares and securities held at 6 April 1965:

- a taxpayer can elect for the capital gains to be calculated by substituting the 6 April 1965 values for the original costs in all cases;

- separate elections must be made for the taxpayer and spouse and they are required both for ordinary shares and for fixed-interest securities;

- the election for each category is irrevocable and has to be made within two years of the end of the tax year in which the first sale after 19 March 1968 occurs;

- if no election is made the capital gain is worked out by comparing the disposal proceeds with the original cost and value of the holding on 6 April 1965.

Where, as is more likely, a taxpayer has elected for the capital gains on disposals of all assets owned on 31 March 1982 to be worked out solely by reference to their values at that date, the above rules setting out the alternatives available for assets held on 6 April 1965 will be superseded.

Valuations

If you need to use any valuations to work out the gain or loss on a disposal, there is a free service from the Inland Revenue to help you to complete your Self-Assessment Tax Return.

You:

- may ask your Tax Office to check valuations after you have made the disposal but before you make your Return;

- can ask for one copy of Form CG34 for each valuation you want checked;

- must then send back the completed form to your Tax Office together with all the other information and documents requested on the form.

If your valuations are agreed they will not subsequently be challenged when you submit your Tax Return unless there are important facts affecting the valuations that you did not mention. If your figures are not agreed the Inland Revenue will put forward alternative valuations.

Your private residence

The profit on a sale of your home is exempt from tax. The exemption extends to the house and its garden or grounds up to half a hectare, including the land on which the house is built. A larger area can qualify for exemption where it can be shown that it was needed to enjoy the house.

Where a home has not been occupied as your private residence throughout the full period of ownership, or, if later, since 31 March 1982, a proportion of the gain on sale becomes taxable. Nevertheless, certain periods of absence are disregarded in determining whether the gain is totally exempt from tax. These are:

- the last three years of ownership in any event; and

- generally those when you have to live away from home because of your work.

Ben White realized a capital gain of £68,000 when he sold his home in December 2003. It had been acquired back in May 1994. He was employed abroad between October 1994 and February 1996. In March 2000 he moved out into his new home.

Both the time spent working overseas and the last three years are regarded as periods when the home was Ben's main residence. The chargeable period is, therefore, only nine months and the chargeable gain, before taper relief, is £5,321 as follows:

$$\frac{\text{Chargeable period}}{\text{Period of ownership}} = \frac{9 \text{ months}}{115 \text{ months}} \times £68,000 = £5,321$$

Where part of your home is used exclusively for business purposes the proportion of the profit on sale attributable to the business use is a chargeable gain. Whether part of your home is actually used exclusively for business use is entirely a matter of fact.

If you let all or part of your home as residential accommodation, the gain on the part which has been let is either wholly or partly exempt from tax. The proportion of the profit on sale which is exempt is the lower of:

- either £40,000; or

- an amount equivalent to the gain on the part you have occupied as your home.

Bill Gray made a capital gain of £94,000 when he disposed of his home in November 2003. It had been bought in June 1997. Bill and his family lived there until October 1997 and from October 2000 up to the date of sale. In the intervening period it was let. This period of absence was not one when the home was still regarded as Bill's main residence.

The chargeable gain is only £3,159 as follows:

	£	£
Capital gain (period of ownership – 77 months)		94,000
Less: Main residence exemption		
– 41 months	50,051	
Letting exemption – 36 months		
(lower of £40,000 or £50,051)	40,000	
		90,051
		3,949
Less: Taper relief – 20%		790
Chargeable gain		£3,159

Alternatively, if you take in lodgers who mix in and eat with your family, the Inland Revenue take the view that no part of the exemption on a sale of your home is lost. Nor should any capital gain arise if you take advantage of the Rent-a-Room scheme mentioned in Chapter 9.

A second home

If you have two homes such as a house or flat in town for use during the weekdays and a cottage in the country for weekends, the profit on sale of only one of them is exempt from tax. Which one counts as your main residence is a matter of fact. It is, however, possible for you to determine this by writing to your tax office. In the election you should request which of your homes you want regarded as your principal private residence for Capital Gains Tax purposes. The election:

• should apply from the date when you first have at least two homes available to you;

• can be made at any time in the two years beginning with the date from which it is to apply;

• can be varied as and when it suits you.

Husband and wife living together are only allowed one qualifying home between them.

If you own a home that was occupied rent free by the same dependent relative both on 5 April 1988 and throughout your period of ownership, then the profit on sale is tax free. Otherwise, it is likely that part of the gain will be taxable.

Chattels

Gains on the sales of chattels with an expected life of more than 50 years sold for less than £6,000 are exempt from tax. Chattels include paintings and other works of art, antiques, furniture, jewellery, stamps and ornaments. Articles comprising a set are regarded as a single item when they are sold to the same person but at different times.

For items which fetch between £6,000 and £15,000 the chargeable gain is restricted to 5/3 times the amount of the proceeds of sale (ignoring expenses) over £6,000 where this is to the taxpayer's advantage.

A piece of antique furniture purchased in January 1989 for £2,300 was sold at auction in June 2003 for £8,700, after expenses of sale were deducted.

The indexation allowance between January 1989 and April 1998 is 0.465.

The chargeable gain is £3,600 as follows:

	£	£
Sale price		8,700
Less: Purchase price	2,300	
Indexation allowance 0.465	1,070	3,370
Gain		£5,330
But restricted to $5/3$ x £2,700 (£8,700 – £6,000)		4,500
Less: Taper Relief – 20%		900
Chargeable gain		£3,600

Where an article is sold at a loss for under £6,000, the allowable loss is restricted by assuming the proceeds on sale were equivalent to £6,000.

A painting was purchased many years ago for £10,400. It was sold in March 2004 for £7,500. The allowable loss is £2,900. If it had fetched £4,000 on sale, the allowable loss would only be £4,400 (£10,400 – £6,000).

Wasting assets

Wasting assets are assets with an expected life span of less than 50 years. Unless it comes within the definition of 'tangible moveable property' a gain on the sale of a wasting asset is calculated in the same way as that on the sale of any other asset, except that the purchase price wastes away during the asset's expected life span. Leases of land for less than 50 years are wasting assets. A specific table is provided for calculating the proportion of the purchase price of a lease that can be deducted from the sale proceeds.

The gain on a sale of a wasting asset that is also 'tangible moveable property' is exempt from tax. Neither does a loss on a sale of similar property count as an allowable loss.

Part disposals

Where you only sell part of an asset:

- its acquisition cost is apportioned between the part sold and the proportion retained. This is done on a pro-rata basis by reference to the proceeds of sale of the part sold and the open-market value of the proportion retained;

- any indexation allowance is calculated on the cost of the part sold;

- the proportion of the original cost of the asset attributable to the part that was not sold can be set against the proceeds on a sale of the remainder at a later date. This calculation must be reworked on the 31 March 1982 value of an asset acquired before that date where the part disposal took place before 6 April 1988;

- if the part sold is small compared with the value of the entire asset or shareholding you can claim to deduct the sale proceeds from the acquisition cost. Where the part disposal is one of land this procedure can be adopted so long as the sale proceeds are both less than £20,000 and one-fifth of the value of the remaining land.

Enterprise Investment Scheme

Any gain on the disposal of qualifying shares under the Enterprise Investment Scheme (EIS) is exempt from Capital Gains Tax, provided:

- The Income Tax relief on the investment has not been withdrawn.

- The disposal takes place at least three years after the issue of the shares.

An investor who suffers a loss on disposing of qualifying shares can offset the loss against either:

- Capital Gains in the year the loss is realized; or

- Taxable income in the year of loss or the previous year.

It is also possible for individuals to defer Capital Gains Tax payable on chargeable gains by reinvesting the gains in qualifying EIS shares. For the purposes of deferral relief the chargeable gains must be reinvested within the period beginning one year before, and ending three years after, the original disposal. Deferral relief can be claimed:

- In conjunction with both Income Tax relief (see Chapter 9) and the exemption from Capital Gains Tax (as above) up to the annual investment limit of £150,000; or

- On its own as there is no limit on the amount of gains that can be deferred; or

- In any other combination within the rules chosen by the investor.

Under deferral relief the original liability to Capital Gains Tax crystallizes when the EIS shares are sold.

Venture Capital Trusts

A disposal of shares in a Venture Capital Trust is free of Capital Gains Tax provided:

- The original cost of the shares disposed of did not exceed £100,000 in any one tax year; and

- The company qualifies as a Venture Capital Trust (VCT) both at the time the shares are acquired and also at the date of disposal.

Like the EIS, a further relief is available for individuals who subscribe for new shares in a VCT, as opposed to purchase from a third party. Those individuals can defer a tax charge on a chargeable gain arising on the disposal of any assets, provided:

- The reinvestment in new shares of a VCT is made in a period beginning one year before, and ending one year after, the original disposal; and

- The maximum annual investment limit of £100,000 for Income Tax relief (see Chapter 9) is not breached.

Tax on the deferred gain will be payable when the shares are sold or in other circumstances.

The legislation dealing with both the EIS and VCTs is both lengthy and complex. It contains a number of conditions and restrictions and, as a result, is yet another area of your tax and financial affairs where you would do well to seek advice from a tax specialist.

Gifts

The capital gain on a gift is calculated by using the market value of the asset at the date of gift. The amount of the gain is reduced by any indexation allowance that is due.

Where the gift is one of business assets you can elect with the transferee for payment of the tax on the gift to be postponed until the asset is subsequently disposed of by the transferee. This same rule also applies in other restricted circumstances. For gifts of some assets where deferral is not available the Capital Gains Tax can be paid in ten equal annual instalments.

Deferred gains on business assets and gifts

Earlier in this chapter you read about the rules for working out the capital gains on assets that you owned at the end of March 1982. In preceding sections I have made mention of postponing the payment of Capital Gains Tax on gifts and the proceeds of sale of business assets that are reinvested in other assets for use in the business.

Without some special form of relief, the benefit of these rules would be denied where a deferral occurred in the period from 31 March 1982 to 5 April 1988, and a charge to Capital Gains Taxes arises thereafter since the disposal is not of an asset owned on 31 March 1982. The remedy provides for a 50% reduction of the deferred gain.

A business asset purchased in 1978 was sold in January 1986. The deferred gain on the sale was £56,000. The replacement asset cost £120,000 and was sold in September 2003 for £180,000. The indexation allowance between January 1986 and April 1998 is 0.689. The chargeable gain is £6,153 as follows:

		£	£
Sale proceeds			180,000
Less:	Purchase price	120,000	
Less:	Deferred gain	56,000	
		64,000	

Add:	50% of postponed gain	28,000	
		92,000	
Indexation allowance			
£92,000 x 0.689		63,388	155,388
			24,612
Less:	Taper relief – 75%		18,459
2003/04 chargeable gain			£6,153

Inheritances

No Capital Gains Tax is payable on the unrealized profits on your assets at the date of your death. When you inherit an asset you acquire it at the value on the date of death of the deceased. Generally, this rule is also applied whenever you become entitled to assets from a trust.

13 COMPLETING THE RETURN AND CALCULATING YOUR TAX

When you collect your post from the doormat you can always pick out your Tax Return from the other letters. It comes at the same time every year in a thin cellophane envelope with the instruction 'Please open immediately'. This book is being published around the date when you can expect to receive your Tax Return asking for information about your income and capital gains for the year ended 5 April 2004, as well as the allowances and reliefs you want to claim in the same year. Everybody gets:

- the standard ten-page Return;

- guidance notes;

- supplementary pages based on his or her tax history;

- a tax calculation guide.

The additional colour-coded supplementary pages specific to the income and gains of the taxpayer are:

1. Employment	Pink
2. Share schemes	Purple
3. Self-employment	Orange
4. Partnership	Turquoise
5. Land and property	Red
6. Foreign income, gains and tax credit relief	Mustard
7. Trusts, settlements and the estates of deceased persons	Brown
8. Capital gains	Blue
9. Non-residence	Green

There are no supplementary pages for UK investment income which is entered on the main Return.

When you receive your Return try to avoid the temptation to put it to one side. There is no advantage in delaying. It is better to get started sooner because you will:

- have more time to get help from the Inland Revenue if you need it;

- have more time to save money for any tax you have to pay;

- find out earlier if you are due a tax refund;

- get a big weight off your mind!!

Start by filling in page 2. This tells you which supplementary pages you will need. These can be obtained by telephoning the Orderline on 0845 9000 404 (open 7 days a week from 8 a.m. to 10 p.m). Alternatively you can send a fax to 0845 9000 604. The supplementary pages come with Notes to help you fill in the pages you requested. Help Sheets and leaflets giving more detailed information about particular tax rules for working out the income or capital gains to be declared on the supplementary pages are referred to in the Notes and are also available from the Orderline.

Then you should decide if you want to calculate your tax or if you want your tax office to do it for you. Remember the deadlines:

30 September 2004

You must send back your completed Tax Return for the year to 5 April 2004 to your tax office by then if you want the Inland Revenue to:

- calculate your tax in time for you to make payment on 31 January 2005; or

- collect tax owing of less than £2,000 through your tax code.

31 January 2005

This date is important for three reasons. By then you must:

- let your tax office have your completed Return;

- pay the balance of any tax you owe for the 2003/04 tax year (unless it is to be collected through your tax code); and

- if appropriate pay your first payment on account for the 2004/05 tax year.

You are now ready to complete the remainder of your Tax Return. Begin by gathering together all the information for the year ended 5 April 2004 on your income, capital gains, reliefs and allowances from the records you have been keeping for the year.

Keeping proper records

For most kinds of income and capital gains you will only need to keep the records given to you by whoever provided that income. This means for those of you

- in employment:

  — your Form P60, a certificate your employer will give you after 5 April (the end of the tax year) showing details of pay and tax deducted;

  — any Form P45 (part 1A), a certificate from an employer showing details of pay and tax from a job you have left;

  — any Form P160 (part 1A) you may have been given when you retire and go on to receive a pension paid by your former employer;

  — your payslips or pay statements;

  — a note of the amount of any tips or gratuities and details of any other taxable receipts. You are advised to record these as soon as possible after you receive them, not simply estimate them at the end of the year;

  — Form P11D or P9D or equivalent information from all the employers you have worked for during the year, showing any benefits-in-kind and expenses payments given to you.

- receiving a UK pension or social security benefits:

  — your Form P60, a certificate which may be given to you by the payer of your occupational pension, showing the amount of your pension and the tax deducted;

  — any other certificate of a pension you received and the tax deducted from it;

  — details given to you by The Department of Work and Pensions (DWP) relating to state pensions, taxable state benefits, statutory sick pay, statutory maternity or paternity pay and the jobseeker's allowance.

- in business or letting property:

  — please refer to Chapter 6 and the section on Records.

- receiving investment income:

  — bank and building society statements or passbooks;

  — statements of interest and any other income received from your savings and investments; for example, an annuity;

  — any tax deduction certificates supplied by your bank or building society;

  — dividend vouchers received from UK companies;

  — unit trust tax vouchers;

  — life insurance chargeable events certificates;

  — details of any income you received from a trust.

It is also sensible to keep details of any exceptional amounts – such as an inheritance or other windfall – which you receive and invest.

- making capital gains or losses:

  — contracts for the purchase or sale of shares, unit trusts, property or other assets;

  — copies of any valuations taken into account in your calculation of capital gains or losses;

  — bills, invoices or other evidence of payment records such as bank statements and cheque stubs for costs you claim for the purchase, improvement or sale of assets;

  — details of any assets you have given away or put into a trust.

- claiming personal allowances, other deductions or reliefs:

  — certificates of interest paid;

  — court orders or other legally binding maintenance agreements;

  — declarations you have made to charities of gifts under Gift Aid;

  — personal pension plan and self-employed premium certificates;

  — a birth certificate for any claim where age is relevant;

  — a marriage certificate where the married couple's allowance is being claimed;

  — notification that you registered as a blind person.

These are some examples of the types of records you would be advised to keep. The list is not exhaustive and does not cover every situation. If you are in any doubt, ask your tax office or Tax Enquiry Centre for advice.

Even if you do not have all the information you need do not let this deter you from preparing your Tax Return and sending it back to your tax office. Of course, you must do all you can to get the information, but if you are unable to provide final figures when the time comes to send off your Tax Return then estimate the missing amounts. Tick box 23.2 on page 9 of your Return and describe in the space provided at 23.5:

- which figures are provisional. You should refer to the appropriate box numbers on your Tax Return or any of the other supplementary pages you have completed;

- why you could not give final figures;

- when you expect to be able to provide your tax office with the correct information.

Your tax office will not normally regard a Tax Return as incomplete just because it contains provisional details of income or capital gains provided you have taken all reasonable measures to obtain the final figures, and you make sure that you send them as soon as they are available.

Completing the Return

You must answer all the questions. If you answer 'Yes' you should fill in the boxes that apply to you, otherwise move on to the next question.

Always

- write only in the space provided using blue or black ink;

- only use numbers when you are asked for amounts;

- do not include pence.

There is just not enough space for me to reproduce all the supplementary pages and the core Tax Return in the Guide. I have therefore decided to reproduce the front of the supplementary page on Employment and most of pages 3 to 10 of the Tax Return.

If you have more than one job you will need to fill in a separate copy of the Employment page for each employment. In box 1.8 enter your before-tax salary or wage from your form P60. Enter the tax deducted by your employer in box 1.11. The amounts of any benefits-in-kind, which are taxable, will have been worked out by your employer and can be

Inland Revenue

Income for the year ended 5 April 2004

EMPLOYMENT

Fill in these boxes first

Name

DAVID JONES

Tax reference

56178 93777

If you want help, look up the box numbers in the Notes.

Details of employer

Employer's PAYE reference - may be shown under 'Inland Revenue office number and reference' on your P60 or 'PAYE reference' on your P45

1.1 195/ F249

1.2 Employer's name
FIELDGATE TEXTILE Co LTD

Date employment started
(only if between 6 April 2003 and 5 April 2004)

1.3 / /

Date employment finished
(only if between 6 April 2003 and 5 April 2004)

1.4 / /

1.5 Employer's address
FLOWERS LANE
FIELD GATE

Postcode TA6 2NZ

Tick box 1.6 if you were a director of the company
1.6

and, if so, tick box 1.7 if it was a close company
1.7

Income from employment

■ **Money** - *see Notes, page EN3*

Before tax

● Payments from P60 (or P45) **1.8** £ 21,000-00

● Payments not on P60, etc. - tips **1.9** £

- other payments (excluding expenses entered below and lump sums and compensation payments or benefits entered overleaf) **1.10** £

Tax deducted

● **Tax deducted** in the UK from payments in boxes 1.8 to 1.10 **1.11** £ 4,371-60

■ **Benefits and expenses** - *see Notes, pages EN3 to EN6. If any benefits connected with termination of employment were received, or enjoyed, after that termination and were from a **former** employer you need to complete Help Sheet IR204, available from the Orderline. Do not enter such benefits here.*

● Assets transferred/ payments made for you **1.12** £

● Vans **1.18** £

● Vouchers, credit cards and tokens **1.13** £

● Interest-free and low-interest loans see Note for box 1.19, page EN5 **1.19** £

● Living accommodation **1.14** £

box 1.20 is not used

● Excess mileage allowances and passenger payments **1.15** £

● Private medical or dental insurance **1.21** £ 400

● Company cars **1.16** £ 1,500

● Other benefits **1.22** £

● Fuel for company cars **1.17** £ 2,160

● Expenses payments received and balancing charges **1.23** £

SA101

INCOME *for the year ended 5 April 2004*

Q10 Did you receive any income from UK savings and investments? **YES** ✓ If yes, tick this box and then fill in boxes 10.1 to 10.26 as appropriate. Include only your share from any joint savings and investments. If not applicable, go to Question 11.

■ *Interest*

● Interest from UK banks or building societies. (Interest from UK Internet accounts should be included) *If you have more than one bank or building society account enter **totals** in the boxes.*

- enter any bank or building society interest that **has not had tax taken off**. (Most of this interest is taxed before you receive it so make sure you should be filling in box 10.1, rather than boxes 10.2 to 10.4.) Enter other types of interest in boxes 10.5 to 10.14 as appropriate.

Taxable amount
10.1 £

- enter details of your **taxed** bank or building society interest. *The Working Sheet on page 10 of your Tax Return Guide will help you fill in boxes 10.2 to 10.4.*

Amount after tax deducted	Tax deducted	Gross amount before tax
10.2 £ 272	**10.3** £ 68	**10.4** £ 340

● Interest distributions from UK authorised unit trusts and open-ended investment companies (dividend distributions go below)

Amount after tax deducted	Tax deducted	Gross amount before tax
10.5 £	**10.6** £	**10.7** £

● National Savings & Investments (other than First Option Bonds and Fixed Rate Savings Bonds and the first £70 of interest from an Ordinary Account)

Taxable amount
10.8 £ 300

● National Savings & Investments First Option Bonds and Fixed Rate Savings Bonds

Amount after tax deducted	Tax deducted	Gross amount before tax
10.9 £ 144	**10.10** £ 36	**10.11** £ 180

● Other income from UK savings and investments (except dividends)

Amount after tax deducted	Tax deducted	Gross amount before tax
10.12 £	**10.13** £	**10.14** £

■ *Dividends*

● Dividends and other qualifying distributions from UK companies

Dividend/distribution	Tax credit	Dividend/distribution plus credit
10.15 £ 396	**10.16** £ 44	**10.17** £ 440

● Dividend distributions from UK authorised unit trusts and open-ended investment companies

Dividend/distribution	Tax credit	Dividend/distribution plus credit
10.18 £ 180	**10.19** £ 20	**10.20** £ 200

● Scrip dividends from UK companies

Dividend	Notional tax	Dividend plus notional tax
10.21 £ 36	**10.22** £ 4	**10.23** £ 40

● Non-qualifying distributions and loans written off

Distribution/Loan	Notional tax	Taxable amount
10.24 £	**10.25** £	**10.26** £

clearly identified from the copy of your form P11D which will be given to you. Enter these benefits and expenses, if appropriate, in boxes 1.12 to 1.23. The reverse of the employment page deals with:

- lump sums and compensation payments;

- foreign earnings;

- expenses you incurred in doing your job;

- repayments of student loans.

If you received income from UK savings and investments tick the 'Yes' box at the top of page 3 of your Tax Return. You then need to complete boxes 10.1 to 10.26 as appropriate. The page is divided into two halves:

- Interest

  Take note that there are two boxes 10.1 and 10.8 which specifically deal with interest you have received from UK banks, building societies or National Savings where no tax has been deducted.

- Dividends

  Dividends on your shareholdings come with counterfoils. These show the amount of the dividend and the accompanying tax credit. It is the total of all of your dividends in the year, and tax credits, which should be entered in boxes 10.15 and 10.16. Add these totals together to get the 'dividend/distribution plus credit' figure to be shown in box 10.17. The same procedure should be followed for all other dividends that you have received including those on your unit trust investments and 'scrip' dividends from UK companies. A 'scrip' dividend is where you take up an offer of shares instead of a cash dividend.

Did you receive a taxable UK pension, retirement annuity or Social Security benefit in 2003/04? If your pension or benefit is taxable and should be included on the Return tick the 'Yes' box at the top of page 4 and fill in boxes 11.1 to 11.14, as appropriate. As with the Employment page the amount of your pension from a previous employer's pension fund, and the tax deducted throughout the year, will also be shown on a form P60 which has been sent to you. If you are drawing the state pension you should declare the amount of your pension for the 52-week period to 5 April 2004. Particularly where the pension is paid quarterly, there will be a small difference between the income you should declare on the Return and the actual pension received during the tax year. Do not include the £10 Christmas Bonus as this is not taxable.

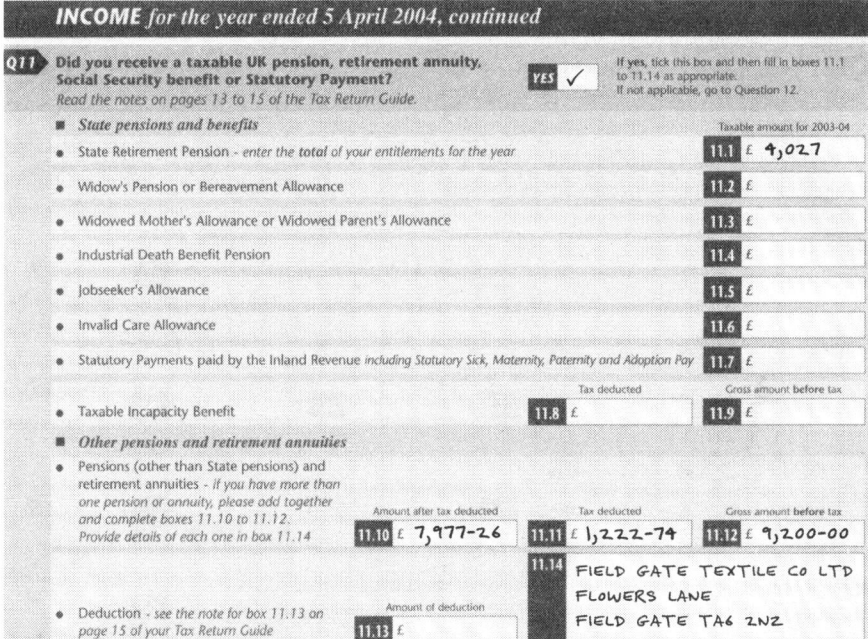

Question 12 will only be of any concern to you if you received any of the following kinds of income:

- gains on UK life insurance policies, life annuities or capital redemption policies;

- refunds of surplus additional voluntary contributions.

If you do not need to tick the 'Yes' box you can go straight to question 13 which asks you whether you received any other income that has not already been entered elsewhere on your Tax Return. This would include, for example:

- any casual earnings not declared elsewhere;

- accrued income on a transfer of securities;

- income received after your business has ceased.

Question 14 is the first in the section dealing with reliefs for the year ended 5 April 2004 and is relevant if you want to claim relief for pension contributions. If:

- you pay into both a retirement annuity contract and a personal pension plan; or

- you bring back into 2003/04 payments made after 5 April 2004; or

- you carry back payments in 2003/04 to a previous year; or

- the figure in box 14.5, or 14.9 is more than the appropriate percentage limit of your earnings;

you must telephone the Orderline and ask for Help Sheet IR 330 Pension Payments, which includes working sheets to help you complete the boxes.

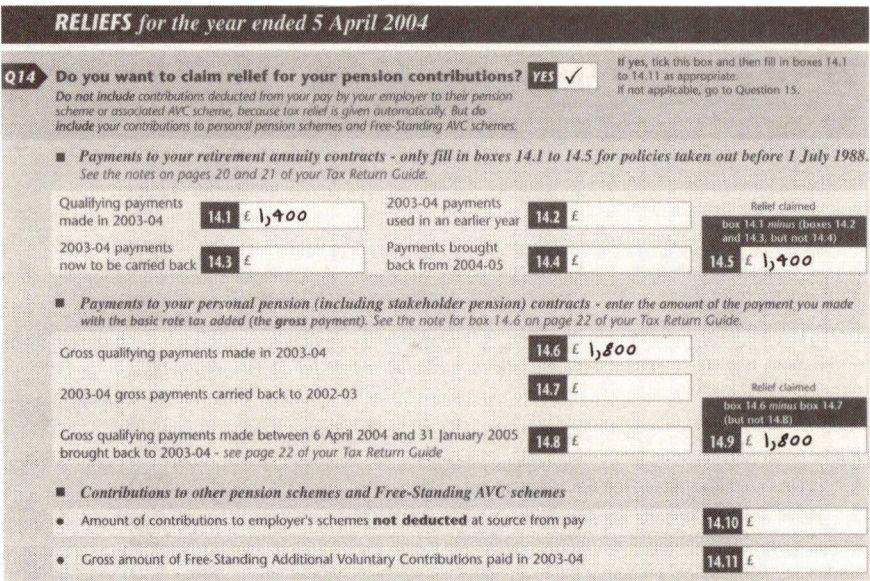

Question 15 lists a number of reliefs. Do you want to claim any of them? They include:

- interest paid on qualifying loans;

- maintenance or alimony payments you are making;

- your subscriptions for new ordinary shares in a Venture Capital Trust;

- subscriptions under the Enterprise Investment Scheme;

- expenses incurred on your business, but after it has ceased trading;

- payments to a trade union or friendly society for death benefits.

You may be entitled to higher-rate tax relief on donations to charities under Gift Aid. Such payments are regarded as having been made by you after tax at the basic rate has been deducted. No further tax relief is due unless you pay tax the the top rate of 40%.

Q15 **Do you want to claim any of the following reliefs?**
If you have made any annual payments, after basic rate tax, answer 'Yes' to Question 15 and fill in box 15.9. If you have made any gifts to charity go to Question 15A.

YES ✓

If yes, tick this box and then fill in boxes 15.1 to 15.12, as appropriate.
If not applicable, go to Question 15A

Amount of payment

- Interest eligible for relief on qualifying loans — **15.1** £ *850*

Amount claimed up to £2,150

- Maintenance or alimony payments you have made under a court order, Child Support Agency assessment or legally binding order or agreement — **15.2** £ *1,780*

To claim this relief, either you or your former spouse must have been 65 or over on 5 April 2000. So, if **your** date of birth, which is entered in box 22.6, is after 5 April 1935 then you must enter your former **spouse's** date of birth in box 15.2A - *see pages 23 and 24 of your Tax Return Guide*

Former spouse's date of birth

15.2A *11/10/31*

Amount on which relief is claimed

- Subscriptions for Venture Capital Trust shares (up to £100,000) — **15.3** £ *6,000*

Amount on which relief is claimed

- Subscriptions under the Enterprise Investment Scheme (up to £150,000) - *also provide details in the 'Additional information' box, box 23.5, see page 24 of your Tax Return Guide* — **15.4** £ *2,250*

- Community Investment Tax relief - invested amount relating to previous tax year(s) and on which relief is due — **15.5** £

Total amount on which relief is claimed
box 15.5 + box 15.6

- Community Investment Tax relief - invested amount for current tax year — **15.6** £ — **15.7** £

- Post-cessation expenses, pre-incorporation losses brought forward and losses on relevant discounted securities, etc. - *see pages 24 and 25 of your Tax Return Guide* — **15.8** £

Amount of payment

Payments made

- Annuities and annual payments — **15.9** £

Half amount of payment

- Payments to a trade union or friendly society for death benefits — **15.10** £

Relief claimed

- Payment to your employer's compulsory widow's, widower's or orphan's benefit scheme - *available in some circumstances – first read the notes on page 25 of your Tax Return Guide* — **15.11** £

Relief claimed

- Relief claimed on a qualifying distribution on the **redemption** of bonus shares or securities. — **15.12** £

ALLOWANCES *for the year ended 5 April 2004*

Q15A **Do you want to claim relief on gifts to charity?**
If you have made any Gift Aid payments answer 'Yes' to Question 15A. You should include Gift Aid payments to Community Amateur Sports Clubs here. You can elect to include in this Return Gift Aid payments made between 6 April 2004 and the date you send in this Return. See page 26 in the Tax Return Guide.

YES ✓

If yes, tick this box and then read page 26 of your Tax Return Guide. Fill in boxes 15A.1 to 15A.7 as appropriate.
If not applicable, go to Question 16.

- Gift Aid payments, including covenanted payments to charities, made between 6 April 2003 and 5 April 2004 — **15A.1** £ *1,600*

- Enter in box 15A.2 the total of any 'one off' payments included in box 15A.1 — **15A.2** £ *1,200*

- Enter in box 15A.3 the amount of Gift Aid payments made after 5 April 2003 but treated as if made in the tax year 2002-03 — **15A.3** £ *600*

- Enter in box 15A.4 the amount of Gift Aid payments made after 5 April 2004 but treated as if made in the tax year 2003-04 — **15A.4** £ *800*

box 15A.1 + box 15A.4 *minus* box 15A.3

- Enter in box 15A.5 the total relief claimed in 2003-04 — **15A.5** £

- Gifts of qualifying investments to charities – shares and securities — **15A.6** £ *2,500*

- Gifts of qualifying investments to charities – real property — **15A.7** £

You should enter in boxes 15A.1 and 15A.2 (as appropriate) the amount of any payments made by you in the year to 5 April 2004, even if you are not claiming higher-rate tax relief. Cash gifts to Community Amateur Sports Clubs, using Gift Aid, are treated in the same way as Gift Aid payments to charity.

Perhaps by the time you complete your Tax Return and send it back to your Tax Office you have made Gift Aid donations in the 2004/05 tax year starting on 6 April 2004. You can elect to have those payments treated as though they were made in the year to 5 April 2004. You can do so by entering the amount of such payments in box 15A.4. Similarly, any payments made in 2003/04 and related back to 2002/03 should be entered in box 15A.3 of the form.

Question 16 is devoted to the allowances for the year ended 5 April 2004 which you may want to claim. There are separate sections covering all the personal allowancesand the individuals – whether they be single, married, or elderly – who can claim them. In each case there is a space for you to enter the information the Inland Revenue need to make sure you are given the full and right tax allowances.

The first part of this section is for you to make a claim for the special blind person's allowance. You will need to give the name of the local authority, or equivalent body, with whom you have registered your blindness as well as the date of registration.

Then comes the section on claiming the married couple's allowance. This can only be claimed if either you, or your husband or wife, were born before 6 April 1935. So you can only claim the allowance in 2003/04 if either of you had reached 65 years of age before 6 April 2000.

The section at the top of page 7 is about transferring surplus allowances.

The remainder of the Return asks for other information for the year ended 5 April 2004 and is all relatively straightforward. When the Return is finished it must be signed and dated in the space provided on page 10. Bear in mind the wording of the declaration: 'The information I have given in this Tax Return is correct and complete to the best of my know-

■ *Married couple's allowance -*

In 2003-04 married couple's allowance can only be claimed if either you, or your husband or wife, were born before 6 April 1935. So you can only claim the allowance in 2003-04 if either of you had reached 65 years of age before 6 April 2000. Further guidance is given beginning on page 27 of your Tax Return Guide.

If **both** you and your husband or wife were born after 5 April 1935 you cannot claim; **do not** complete boxes 16.3 to 16.13.

If **you can claim** fill in boxes 16.3 and 16.4 if you are a married man or if you are a married woman and you are claiming half or all of the married couple's allowance.

- Enter your date of birth (if born before 6 April 1935) **16.3** | 12 / 02 / 33

- Enter your spouse's date of birth (if born before 6 April 1935 **and** if older than you) **16.4** | 25 / 09 / 21

Then, if you are a married man fill in boxes 16.5 to 16.9. If you are a married woman fill in boxes 16.10 to 16.13.

- Wife's full name **16.5** | WENDY MARTIN | • Date of marriage (if after 5 April 2003) **16.6** | / /

- Tick box 16.7, or box 16.8, if you or your wife have allocated half, or all, of the minimum amount of the allowance to her | Half All | **16.7** ✓ **16.8**

- Enter in box 16.9 the date of birth of any previous wife with whom you lived at any time during 2003-04. Read *'Special rules if you are a man who married in the year ended 5 April 2004'* on page 28 before completing box 16.9. **16.9** | / /

- Tick box 16.10, or box 16.11, if you or your husband have allocated half, or all, of the minimum amount of the allowance to you | Half All | **16.10** **16.11**

- Husband's full name **16.12** | • Date of marriage (if after 5 April 2003) **16.13** | / /

ledge and belief'. Then send the form back to your tax office. As there is no space in each section of the Return you may well need to prepare separate statements of, for example, your interest and dividend income in order to arrive at the single figures which need to be entered on the Return. I strongly recommend that copies of any supporting statements or schedules which you prepare should be sent to your tax office along with the Return. Do not, however, send in any building society statements, dividend vouchers and other financial records. Just keep them safely.

If, after you have sent off your Tax Return, you find that you have made a mistake, let your tax office know at once so that it can be taken into account.

Calculating your tax

You should receive a Tax Calculation Guide with your Tax Return. This will help you if you want to calculate your tax. If your tax affairs are more complicated you will need to ask for the Comprehensive Tax Calculation Guide. The key steps in calculating your tax bill are as follows:

- bring together all the non-savings income you have entered on your Return;

- total the deductions and allowances you have claimed for the year;

- add your savings and dividend income to arrive at your total income, take away your deductions and allowances to get your taxable income, then work out the tax due, so far;

- take off further allowances, deductions and tax paid at source – then work out your total Income Tax, Class 4 National Insurance Contributions (if you are self-employed or in partnership) and any Student Loan Repayments – to give you the figure to enter in box 18.3 on page 7 of your Return;

- work out what you have to pay for 2003/04 by 31 January 2005;

- calculate any 2004/05 payments on account you may have to make on 31 January and 31 July 2005.

George Salmon is employed by a local company as a senior engineer. Since the beginning of July 1997 he has regularly been asked to speak at seminars and write articles for trade magazines. George is 53 (he was born on 8 February 1951) and is happily married to Lynne. They do not have any children. He owns a modest number of investments and his spare cash is deposited in National Savings and building society accounts.

George files his Tax Return for the year to 5 April 2004 on 22 October 2004. It shows the following entries:

	£	Box Number in Return
(1) Employment		
Salary	38,000.00	1.8
Tax deducted by employer	10,220.80	1.11
Subscription to the Association of Mechanical Engineers	100.00	1.34
Company car benefit	3,700.00	1.16
Fuel benefit for company car	2,880.00	1.17
(2) Self-Employment		
Adjusted profit shown by the accounts for the year to 30 June 2003	10,000.00	3.92

George applied for, and was granted, permission to defer payment of Class 4 National Insurance Contributions

Tax payments of £1,300 have been made on both 31 January 2004 and 31 July 2004 based on George's tax liability for 2002/03

Personal pension premiums paid in 2003/04 (based on self-employed earnings and paid gross)	2,500.00	14.9
(3) Savings Income		
National Savings Income Bonds (paid gross)	250.00	10.8
Building Society interest received		
– gross interest	600.00	10.4
– tax deducted	120.00	10.3
– net interest	480.00	10.2
Dividends from share investments		
– gross	1,500.00	10.17
– tax credit	150.00	10.16
– dividends	1,350.00	10.15
(4) Reliefs		
In the year George paid £312 (equivalent to £400 before tax) under Gift Aid to the Cancer Research Campaign		15A.1

Unfortunately, the Inland Revenue's Tax Calculation Guide runs to a substantial number of pages and there is insufficient space to reproduce them here. An abbreviated version of George Salmon's tax calculation is as follows:

	£	£
Employment		
Salary and taxable benefits	44,580	
Less: Professional subscription	100	
		44,570
Self-employment		10,000
UK interest (before tax)		
Interest from UK building society	600	
National Savings interest paid gross	250	
		850
UK dividends and tax credits		1,500

Total income	**57,100**

Deductions for:

Self-employed contributions to personal pension plans	2,500
Gift Aid payment	400
Total deductions	2,900
Total income less deductions	54,200

Allowances given as deduction from income:

Personal allowance	4,615
Net Income Chargeable to Tax	49,585

Tax thereon:

Non-savings income at starting rate, £1,960 at 10%	196.00
Non-savings income at basic rate, £28,540 at 22%	6,278.80
Non-savings income at higher rate, £16,735 at 40%	6,694.00
Savings income (excluding dividends) at higher savings rate, £850 at 40%	340.00
Dividends at higher dividend rate, £1,500 at 32.5%	487.50
	13,996.30

Allowances and reliefs given in terms of tax:

Non-repayable tax credits on dividends	(150.00)
Income tax due after allowances and reliefs	13,846.30
Recoverable tax on Gift Aid payment	88.00
Tax deducted at source from personal pension premiums	550.00
Income tax	**14,484.30**

Tax paid at source:

On salary	(10,220.80)
On UK savings	(120.00)
Income Tax due for 2003/04	**4,143.50**

TAX PAYMENTS

Tax due for 2003/04 (as above)	4,143.50
Payment on account made 31 January 2004	(1,300.00)
Payment on account made 31 July 2004	(1,300.00)
Balance due for 2003/04	1,543.50
Add: First payment on account for 2004/05	2,071.75
Amount due on 31 January 2005	3,615.25
Second payment on account for 2004/05	2,071.75
Amount due on 31 July 2005	2,071.75

From his tax calculation George will then be able to fill in question 18 of his Tax Return as follows:

Q18	Do you want to calculate your tax and, if appropriate, any Student Loan Repayment?	YES ✓	Use your Tax Calculation Guide then fill in boxes 18.1 to 18.8 as appropriate.
•	Underpaid tax for earlier years included in your tax code for 2003-04	**18.1** £	
•	Underpaid tax for 2003-04 included in your tax code for 2004-05	**18.2** £	
•	Student Loan Repayment due	**18.2A** £	
•	Class 4 NIC due	**18.2B** £	
•	Total tax, Class 4 NIC and Student Loan Repayment due for 2003-04 **before** you made any payments on account *(put the amount in brackets if an overpayment)*	**18.3** £ 4,143·50	
•	Tax due calculated by reference to earlier years - *see the notes on page 10 of your Tax Calculation Guide (SA151W)*	**18.4** £	
•	Reduction in tax due calculated by reference to earlier years - *see the notes on page 10 of your Tax Calculation Guide (SA151W)*	**18.5** £	
•	Tick box 18.6 if you are claiming to reduce your 2004-05 payments on account. Make sure you enter the **reduced** amount of your first payment in box 18.7. Then, in the 'Additional information' box, box 23.5 on page 9, say why you are making a claim	**18.6**	
•	Your first payment on account for 2004-05 *(include the pence)*	**18.7** £ 2,071·75	
•	Any 2004-05 tax you are reclaiming now	**18.8** £	

What the Inland Revenue does

When your completed Tax Return is received by your tax office it will be processed as quickly as possible based on your figures. Any simple mistakes will be corrected right away and you will be told about them. This may simply be because your figures do not add up.

If you want to claim a repayment because you have paid too much tax you should answer 'Yes' to Q19. You can, if you want, nominate a charity to receive all or part of your repayment. To do so you will need to answer Q19A appropriately. Information on how to go about this can be found on page 29 of your Tax Return Guide. But if you want to receive your tax repayment personally tick 'Yes' to Q19B and provide the information requested.

You will be sent a calculation of your tax position if you have asked the Inland Revenue to do it for you. If you have worked out your own tax bill, and it is wrong, you will also be advised of the mistakes you have made.

Once your Tax Return has been processed it will be checked. The Inland Revenue have 12 months from 31 January 2005 to check your Tax Return for the year ended 5 April 2004 (longer if you are late in submitting your Return). Remember that enquiries may be made into your figures and you may be asked by your tax office to send in your records in support of them.

Online Filing

This is something that will come to us all one day and it saves the Inland Revenue (and, therefore, taxpayers in general) time and money. The difference in reality is that the Return is filed by the touch of a button rather than the lick of a stamp.

In order to use this service you will need to register with the government gateway, a link to which can be found on the Inland Revenue Home Page www.inlandrevenue.gov.uk. After a few days a user name and password will be sent to you by post, allowing you access to your own area within the Inland Revenue website. Here, you will also be able to view your statement of account showing the amount you owe, or are due back from, your accounts office.

In order to complete your Tax Return you will need to choose your software from a selection of authorised software houses. Alternatively you can use the Inland Revenue's own software. Once downloaded, and in some cases paid for, you are ready to begin work.

Depending on the software chosen the form is completed either directly, as you would the paper version, or via a question and answer session. Some software allows both methods and others build in rather useful checking routines.

14 TAX PAYMENTS, INTEREST, SURCHARGES AND PENALTIES

Two further features of Self-Assessment are:

- one set of payment dates for tax not paid at source;

- a clear statement of your 'account' with the Inland Revenue, showing tax payments both made and due.

Tax payments

Taxpayers with tax to pay on their Self-Assessment must pay the tax due by 31 January following the end of the tax year covered by the Return. The one exception to this rule deals with employees or pensioners who submit their Returns to their tax office by 30 September following the end of the tax year. If the tax they owe is less than £2,000 they can opt to have it collected through the PAYE system.

> Jean Wilkinson sends her 2003/04 Tax Return to her tax office on 26 June 2004. The Inland Revenue calculate she owes tax of £380 for the year. She decides to pay the amount due through the PAYE system. The allowances in her notice of coding for 2005/06 will be restricted to collect the liability month by month throughout the year.

Some taxpayers – mainly the self-employed – will also make two payments on account for the tax year before the Return for that year needs to be submitted. These payments on account are due on:

- 31 January in the tax year; and

- 31 July following the end of the tax year.

If you work out your own tax you will also calculate your own payments on account. Normally you will split into two equal parts the tax paid in the previous tax year (after taking off tax paid at source and any Capital Gains Tax) and pay one half on 31 January and the second instalment six months later at the end of July. However, if you ask your tax office to work out your tax then they will also let you know if you have to make payments on account, and for how much.

You will not need to make payments on account:

- if your liability to Income Tax and Class 4 National Insurance Contributions for the previous tax year – after deducting tax suffered at source on, for example, dividends and building society interest – is less than £500; or

- if more than 80% of your liability to Income Tax and Class 4 National Insurance Contributions for the previous tax year was satisfied by tax paid at source;

- for Capital Gains Tax.

These tests mean that most employees and pensioners who complete Returns will not have to make payments on account under Self-Assessment.

Perhaps, because of a change in your circumstances, the calculation of your payments on account for the year (based, of course, on your tax liability for the previous year) seems likely to overstate your liability for the year.

This might happen if you expect:

- Your income in 2004/05 to be lower than your income in 2003/04.

- Your allowances or reliefs to be higher.

- That more of your income will be taxed at source in 2004/05, because:

    — it will be taxed under PAYE; or

    — your income from savings, for example, interest on bank or building society deposits taxed at source, will increase.

You can then claim to reduce your payments on account. This should be done by using Form SA303, which is available from any tax office. The form also gives you guidance on how to fill it in. When completed, send it back to your tax office.

If your claim to reduce your payments on account subsequently turns out to be excessive then you will be asked to pay interest on the difference between the tax actually paid to your Accounts Office and the amounts that should have been paid.

The tax payment dates for 2003/04 are:

	Due date for *Tax Payments* *on Account*	*Due date for* *Final Balance*
Rental income and untaxed investment income		
Business profits	50% 31/01/2004	31/01/2005
Underpaid PAYE		
(where not coded)	50% 31/07/2004	
Higher Rate Tax on investment income (taxed at source)		
Capital Gains Tax	N/A	31/01/2005

Statements of Account

Under Self-Assessment, taxpayers get statements showing their account with the Inland Revenue, the main features of which are:

- the total tax payable is shown near the top of the statement, below the address. If no tax is due this will also be shown;

- the statement includes a final total line so that it is possible to work through the detailed entries and reconcile these with the total tax payable;

- in most instances the amount payable will be printed on the accompanying payslip.

If you are making payments on account you can expect to receive the following statements up to February 2005:

July 2004	To remind you of the second payment on account for 2003/04 due on 31 July.
August 2004	To tell you of any outstanding balance of the second payment on account. The statement will also include an amount for interest due to date.
January 2005	To advise you of your balancing payment for 2003/04 and your first payment on account for 2004/05, both due on 31 January 2005.
February 2005	To show any outstanding amounts of your Self-Assessment for 2003/04 and your first

> payment on account for 2004/05. The statement
> will also include a charge for interest due to date.

Taxpayers who do not need to make payments on account will not, of course, receive so many statements of account from their tax office. If you are late in paying your tax you will receive additional statements each month.

Paying your tax

If you pay your tax by post, send the payslip and your cheque, both unfolded, in the envelope provided to your Accounts Office. The Inland Revenue politely requests that you do not staple or attach paperclips to cheques. You can help your Accounts Office deal promptly with a payment from you by:

- including a separate letter if you are sending a post-dated cheque, or want to give further information about your payment;

- paying on time – you will then avoid incurring interest charges.

Do not send cash through the post.

You can also pay by one of the other following methods:

- internet or telephone banking;

- bank giro;

- at a post office;

- Girobank;

- debit card (Switch, Solo or Visa Delta) by calling 0845 305 1000 and quoting your Unique Taxpayer Reference.

You can provide for the payment of a future tax liability by purchasing a certificate of tax deposit. Certificates can be bought from the Collector of Taxes. They earn interest from the date of purchase up until the normal due date for payment of the liability. The interest is taxable.

Date of payment

The effective times of receipt of tax are as follows:

Payment Method	*Effective Date of Payment*
Handed in at Inland Revenue office or received by post (except below)	day of receipt by the Inland Revenue
Received by post following a day when the office has been closed for whatever reason (including a weekend)	the day the office was first closed (for payments received on Monday, the effective date will be the previous Saturday)
Electronic Funds Transfer (EFT) – payment by BACS or CHAPS (Clearing House Automated Payment System)	one working day immediately before the date that the value is received. (A working day is defined as a Bank of England working day.)
Bank Giro or Girobank	three working days prior to the date of processing by the Inland Revenue

Interest

If you delay paying your tax you will be charged interest. This applies to both payments on account and balancing payments. The rate of interest is worked out on a set formula. It is an average of the base rates of six main banks (rounded to the nearest whole number) plus 2.5%. At the time of going into print the rate is 6.5%. The interest is calculated from the due date up until payment. You cannot claim tax relief on the interest.

You need to be aware of the circumstances when the imposition of interest would clearly be unfair and can be justifiably contested. The Inland Revenue Code of Practice entitled 'Mistakes by the Inland Revenue' suggests that an Inspector will waive interest if delays have occurred for more than six months over and above the 28-day target of dealing with such matters. The booklet goes on:

'If there is no good reason for a delay, and we have taken more than six months in total – over and above the twenty-eight day target we have set ourselves we will, for amounts unpaid, or not repaid, because of our delay:

- Give up interest that arose on unpaid tax during the period of our delay; or

- Pay you interest (called 'repayment interest') on money we owed you during the period of our delay; and

- Pay any reasonable costs which you have incurred as a direct result of our delay.'

You will be paid interest on any overpayments of the following:

- payments on account of Income Tax;

- Income Tax and Capital Gains Tax paid;

- surcharges on late payment of tax;

- any penalties imposed.

The interest, called repayment supplement, is not taxable. The rate of interest is worked out by first of all taking 1% off the average base rate mentioned above. The resulting figure is then further reduced by the 20% rate of Income Tax deducted at source from savings income. At the time of going into print the rate of repayment supplement is 2.5%.

Remission of tax

Collection of arrears of Income Tax or Capital Gains Tax may be waived if the arrears result from the Inland Revenue's failure to make proper and timely use of information supplied by:

- the taxpayer about his or her own income, capital gains or personal circumstances;

- an employer, where the information affects an employee's notice of coding; or

- the DWP about a taxpayer's retirement, disability or widow's State Pension.

The concession is normally only given where the taxpayer:

- could reasonably have believed that his or her tax affairs were in order; and

- is notified of the arrears by the end of the tax year following that in which it arose.

Surcharges

With Self-Assessment come surcharges. They will be levied automatically on late payment of Capital Gains Tax or the final amount of Income Tax owing as follows:

Tax unpaid by 28 February (one month after the tax was due)	5% of unpaid tax
Tax unpaid by 31 July (six months after the tax was due)	Further 5% of tax unpaid

Notice of any surcharge must be served on you formally by the Inland Revenue. You do have the right to appeal within 30 days if you think you have a reasonable excuse. You might be successful with your appeal if there is clear evidence that your cheque was lost in the post or in the event of serious illness. Lack of funds, apart from exceptional circumstances, or cheques wrongly made out are examples of cases when your appeal would be rejected.

The Inland Revenue booklet SA/BK5 contains examples of what the Inland Revenue will regard as a reasonable excuse for appealing against a surcharge for the late payment of tax.

Penalties

The main penalties under Self-Assessment are:

Offence	Penalty
You do not submit your Tax Return to your Tax Office by 31 January after the end of the tax year	£100
Your Return is still outstanding after a further six months	Further £100

The above penalties are automatic but will be reduced if the tax owing is less. Up to £60 per day in further penalties can be levied on application to the Commissioners by the Inland Revenue.

If taxpayers have a genuinely good excuse for missing the annual 31 January deadline for submitting Tax Returns, they can appeal against the automatic £100 late filing penalty.

Examples of what may be accepted by the Inland Revenue as a reasonable excuse include:

- Where the Tax Return was not received by the taxpayer.

- Where the Tax Return was lost in the post or delayed because of:

  — fire or flood at the Post Office where the Tax Return was handled;

  — prolonged industrial action within the Post Office;

  — an unforeseen event which disrupted the postal services;

- Where a taxpayer lost his or her tax records as a result of fire, flood or theft.

- Serious illness.

- Death of a spouse, domestic partner or close relative.

Examples of what the Inland Revenue will not agree as a reasonable excuse include:

- Tax Return too difficult.

- Pressure of work.

- Lack of information.

- Absence of reminders from the Inland Revenue.

Offence	*Penalty*
Returns still outstanding after the anniversary of the filing date	£200 and a further sum up to the amount of the tax payable
You don't receive a Tax Return and fail to notify the Inland Revenue of chargeability to tax within six months of the end of the tax year	Not exceeding the tax due
Fraudulently or negligently delivering an incorrect Tax Return	Up to the amount of the difference between the tax actually payable and that which was shown as due

Not notifying the Inland Revenue that you have started up in business within 3 months after the end of the month in which you commenced your self-employment	£100
Failure to produce documents during an Inland Revenue enquiry	An initial penalty of £50 followed by a further penalty of up to £30 for each day during which the failure continues
Failure to maintain and keep records	Up to £3,000
Fraudulently or negligently claiming to reduce interim tax payments	Up to an amount equivalent to the difference between the tax paid and the tax that should have been paid

Generally a penalty determination must be made, or proceedings commenced, within six years of the date on which the penalty was incurred. The rules allow for this to be extended to any later time within three years of the final determination of the tax liability.

15 ELECTIONS AND CLAIMS – TIME LIMITS

You will already have gathered that certain options available to you as a taxpayer are dependent on you submitting an election or claim to the appropriate authority. As these will usually involve a saving in tax it is important to appreciate that you often need to act within prescribed time limits. This chapter brings together those elections and claims that are most likely to concern you. It also sets out the time available during which they must be submitted to the Inspector of Taxes or Customs and Excise. It is by no means exhaustive.

Chapter 2 – Tax Rates, Allowances and Credits

Election/Claim	*Time Limit*
The various elections for the transfer of the married couple's and blind person's allowances	Generally before the start of the tax year for which it is to have effect
Claim to the personal allowances detailed in the chapter	No later than five years after 31 January next following the end of the tax year
Transfer of excess allowances between husband and wife	No later than five years after 31 January next following the end of the tax year
Claims for Tax Credits	Claims will only be backdated by a maximum of three months

Chapter 5 – Value Added Tax

Election/Claim	*Time Limit*
Application for Registration	No later than 30 days from the end of the month after the one when turnover exceeds the registration limit
Submission to Customs and Excise of each VAT Return with full payment of the tax due	Within one month after the end of the VAT accounting period
Claim for Bad Debt Relief	When a debt remains unpaid for more than six months

Chapter 6 – The Self-Employed

Election/Claim	*Time Limit*
Relief for post-cessation expenses	No later than one year after 31 January next following the tax year in which the payments are made
Creating a separate pool to work out the capital allowances on an asset with a short life expectancy	No later than one year after 31 January next following the tax year in which the period of account ended in which the expenditure is incurred
Relief for the loss sustained in the the tax year against other income of the same year or the preceding year	Within one year after 31 January next following the tax year in which the loss arose
Relief for a trading loss against the profits arising from the same trade in subsequent periods	Within five years after 31 January next following the tax year in which the loss was sustained
Relief for the loss in the first four years of assessment of a new business to be given against the income of the three preceding years of assessment	No later than one year after 31 January next following the tax year in which the loss occurred
Relief for trading losses to be offset against Capital Gains	No later than one year after 31 January next following the tax year
Relief for the loss in the last 12 months of trading to be given against the profits of the same trade which were assessed in the three tax years prior to the year in which the trade was discontinued	Within five years after 31 January next following the tax year in which the trade ceased

Chapter 8 – Personal Pensions

Election/Claim	*Time Limit*
Personal and stakeholder pension contributions to be treated as paid in the preceding year of assessment	The contributions must be paid by 31 January following the end of the tax year. The claim must be made when, or before, the premium is paid

Retirement annuity premiums to be treated as paid in the preceding year of assessment	By 31 January after the tax year in which payment was made

Chapter 9 – Investment Income

Election/Claim	*Time Limit*
An election to opt out of the Rent-a-Room relief for a particular tax year, or withdrawal of an election	Within one year after 31 January next following the tax year
An election for the alternative basis of Rent-a-Room relief, or revocation of an election	Within one year after 31 January next following the tax year
Claim for Income Tax relief under the Enterprise Investment Scheme	Within five years after 31 January next following that in which the shares were issued
Declaration by a married couple that their beneficial interest in joint property and the income arising from it are unequal	The date of the declaration which must be sent to the Inland Revenue within 60 days

Chapter 12 – Capital Gains Tax

Election/Claim	*Time Limit*
Claim to the capital loss where the value of an asset becomes negligible	The loss arises on the date of claim although, in practice, a two-year period is allowed from the end of the tax year in which the asset became of negligible value
Claim for the loss on shares that were originally subscribed for in an unquoted trading company to be set against income in the year of loss, or the preceding year	No later than one year after 31 January next following the tax year in which the loss was made
An election for the capital gains on disposals of assets you owned on 31 March 1982 to be worked out by reference to their values on that date, ignoring original costs	Within one year after 31 January next following the tax year in which the first disposal of an asset you owned on 31 March 1982 takes place

Claim for the 6 April 1965 value to be substituted in a calculation of the capital gain arising on the sale of an asset held at that date	No later than one year after 31 January next following the tax year in which the disposal is made
An election to determine which of your homes is to be regarded as your principal residence for Capital Gains Tax purposes	Two years from the date when two or more properties are eligible
Disposal of assets and reinvestment of gain in qualifying company	Within five years after 31 January next following the tax year to which it relates
Claim to roll-over relief on the disposal of business assets	No later than five years after 31 January next following the tax year to which it relates
Claim to a reduction in the deferred gain on assets acquired in the period 31 March 1982 to 5 April 1988	Within one year after 31 January next following the tax year in which the disposal takes place

16 INHERITANCE TAX

Not only might Inheritance Tax be payable on transfers or gifts you make during your lifetime, but it is also due on the value of your estate on death. Husband and wife are treated as separate individuals, and both are entitled to the various exemptions. Inheritance Tax is far from straightforward. What follows is a brief outline. The Tax is administered by the Capital Taxes Office, to whom all Returns and Accounts should be submitted.

Potentially exempt transfers

The most significant feature of Inheritance Tax is the concept of a potentially exempt transfer (PET). This is:

- an outright gift to an individual;

- a gift into an accumulation-and-maintenance settlement;

- a gift into a settlement for the benefit of a disabled person;

- a gift into an interest in possession trust;

- the termination of an interest in possession settlement where the settled property passes to an individual, an accumulation-and-maintenance settlement, or a trust for the benefit of a disabled person.

No tax is payable provided the donor lives for at least seven years after making the gift. A form of tapering relief applies where death occurs within seven years. The amount of Inheritance Tax is then calculated at the rates that apply at the date of death as shown in the following table:

Number of Years between Gift and Death	% of Tax Payable
Not more than 3	100
Between 3 and 4	80
Between 4 and 5	60
Between 5 and 6	40
Between 6 and 7	20

Suppose, however, the PET is within the limit of chargeable transfers taxable at a nil rate. There will then be no benefit from tapering relief as no Inheritance Tax is payable on the PET.

Gifts with reservation

If you make a gift but continue to enjoy some benefit from it, the property or asset you have given away is likely to be treated as yours until either the date when you cease to enjoy any benefit from the gift, or your death. This is a 'gift with reservation'. For example, you give your house to your children but continue to live there, rent free. Your house would then be counted as part of your estate and the seven-year period would not start until you either moved home or began to pay a commercial rent.

Lifetime gifts

If you make a gift during your lifetime which is not a potentially exempt transfer it will attract liability to Inheritance Tax at one half of the rates that apply on death. An example of such a lifetime gift is a transfer into a discretionary trust.

Exemptions

The main exemptions applicable to individuals are:

- transfers between husband and wife, during lifetime and on death;

- gifts up to £3,000 in any one tax year. Any part of the exemption that is left over can be carried forward to the following year only. For example, if your total transfers came to £1,200 during 2002/03 you could have given away as much as £4,800 during 2003/04 all within your annual exemption limit. However, if your gifts totalled £3,000 in 2002/03, you would be limited to £3,000 in 2003/04 as well;

- gifts to any one person up to £250 per person in each tax year. Where the total amount given to any one individual exceeds this limit no part comes within this exemption;

- marriage gifts. The amount you can give away in consideration of marriage depends on your relationship to the bride or groom, as follows:

	£
By either parent	5,000
By a grandparent or great-grandparent	2,500
By any other person	1,000

- regular gifts out of income which form part of your normal expenditure;
- gifts to charities and 'qualifying' political parties, both without limit. Both these exceptions apply to lifetime gifts and to bequests on death;
- lump sums paid out of your Pension Scheme on death. The trustees should have discretion over who receives the cash payments.

Business property

Subject to certain conditions, qualifying business assets and interests in businesses qualify for relief for transfers arising either in lifetime or on death. There are two rates:

100% for:

- unincorporated businesses;
- all holdings of unquoted shares in qualifying companies.

50% for:

- shares giving control of a quoted company;
- land, buildings, machinery or plant used in a partnership or controlled company where the transferor is a partner or controlling shareholder.

Unquoted shares include those traded on the Alternative Investment Market (AIM).

Agricultural property

The reliefs applying to agricultural land and holdings are similar to those for business property. Subject to certain minimum ownership and use conditions, the two rates are again:

100% for:

- land and buildings where the transferor has vacant possession, or the right to obtain it, within 12 months;

- agricultural property let for periods exceeding 12 months where the letting commenced on or after 1 September 1995.

50% for:

- other qualifying property.

Trusts

There are special provisions covering the application of Inheritance Tax to different types of Trust. Perhaps the three most common forms of trust are:

- Interest in Possession Trusts where someone is entitled to the trust income as and when it arises. For Inheritance Tax purposes the person so entitled is deemed to own the trust assets personally;

- Discretionary Trusts, where both income and capital are distributed to the beneficiaries at the discretion of the trustees. There are complex rules for computing the liabilities that can arise when assets pass from the trust to beneficiaries. A further charge arises on the assets in the trust on each tenth anniversary from its commencement;

- Accumulation and Maintenance Trusts, which, generally, provide for young members of a family. To qualify under this category the trust must provide that someone will become entitled to either the capital or the income of the trust by the age of 25. Until then no interest in possession must exist. For such qualifying trusts, no charge to Inheritance Tax arises when the beneficiaries become entitled.

Rates of tax

Each taxable gift or transfer is not considered in isolation in calculating how much tax is payable on it. In working out how much is payable, previous taxable transfers are taken into account. This is because the tax due on each chargeable gift or the value of your estate on death is dependent upon the cumulative value of all other chargeable transfers in the seven years leading up to the date of the next chargeable transfer. The rates payable on death from 6 April 2003 are:

Band (£)	Rate %
0–255,000	0
Over 255,000	40

These rates also apply to all lifetime gifts or transfers within three years of death. Inheritance Tax payable on PETS more than three years before but within seven years of death is determined by the first table in this chapter.

The limit of £255,000 on chargeable transfers taxable at a nil rate is increased each year in the same way as for personal Income Tax allowances and tax bands.

Death

When somebody dies, their assets pass to their estate. The estate is then administered by their personal representatives, whose main duties are to:

- gather in the assets left by the deceased individual;
- settle their debts;
- pay out any legacies, and then
- distribute any remaining assets to the beneficiaries.

On a death an Inheritance Tax Return form is completed and submitted together with an application for a Grant of:

- probate where there is a will; or
- administration where there is no will.

The Return must be lodged within 12 months of the date of death. It must include information about previous transfers and gifts which are required to work out the amount of Inheritance Tax payable. Therefore, you are well advised to maintain complete records of your lifetime gifts. Also, to help your executors you should maintain up-to-date details of all your assets and where the supporting certificates and documents are stored.

Usually it is not necessary to submit a Return where the deceased's estate does not exceed £240,000.

As with your annual Tax Return there are penalties for late Returns, delays, negligence or fraud.

Wendy Brown, a widow, died on 30 September 2003 leaving her entire estate to her daughter. She did not make any gifts in the seven years leading up to her death. Her assets and unpaid bills on her death were:

Assets	Value	
	£	£
Flat	200,000	
Household effects	2,000	
Car	5,000	
Building society account	30,000	
Shares	40,000	
Current account	2,500	
		279,500
Less: Allowable Deductions		
Funeral expenses	920	
Income Tax	500	
Telephone bill	50	
Electricity bill	60	
		1,530
Net Value of Estate		£277,970
Inheritance Tax Payable		
On first £255,000		Nil
On next £22,970 at 40%		£9,188
		£9,188

The tax is payable out of Wendy Brown's estate by the executors of her will.

Sales at a loss

Relief is available where certain assets are sold during specified periods after death for less than the valuation at the date of death.

• In the case of land and buildings, the period is four years.

• For quoted securities the time limit is one year.

The relief is available to 'the appropriate person' (the one who pays the tax). All sales by that person in the respective periods must be aggregated. As a result, losses may accordingly be reduced or eliminated by profits so that the relief could be restricted or lost. When this type of relief is due, the net proceeds of sale are substituted for the valuation at death. The Inheritance Tax liability is then recalculated.

Payment of tax

The persons primarily liable for payment of Inheritance Tax are:

• the transferor in respect of chargeable lifetime gifts;

• the personal representatives on death.

There is a process that allows personal representatives to draw on funds held in a deceased's bank and building society accounts solely for the purpose of paying any Inheritance Tax that is due before the Grant of Probate can be issued.

The due dates for payment are:

• for chargeable lifetime gifts – six months after the end of the month in which the gift was made;

• for potentially exempt transfers which become chargeable on death, and the charge on death itself – six months after the end of the month in which the death occurred.

There is an option to pay the tax on certain types of assets by ten equal annual instalments. The first payment is due on the normal due date.

The relevant assets are:

- land and buildings;

- controlling shareholdings;

- unquoted shares, subject to certain conditions;

- businesses.

In the case of lifetime transfers which are, or become, chargeable, the instalment option is only available if the tax is borne by the transferee. Where the asset is sold during the instalment paying period, outstanding instalments become payable immediately.

Interest is payable on Inheritance Tax liabilities from the due date until the date of payment. At the time of going to print the rate of interest is 3%. Where the instalment option is in force, no interest is payable on the outstanding instalments except on:

- land and buildings which do not qualify for business property or agricultural property relief;

- shares and securities in investment companies.

Intestacy

If you die without having made a will your estate will be divided up under the statutory intestacy rules. If you are married and survived by both your spouse and children, your spouse is entitled to a statutory legacy of £125,000. This increases to £200,000 if there are no children but you are survived by specific relatives.

The present intestacy rules for individuals who die domiciled in England or Wales can be summarized as follows:

Unmarried individual

Survived by

Children or grandchildren
Parents
Brothers and sisters
Half-brothers and half-sisters
Grandparents
Uncles and aunts
The Crown

The total estate is shared in the following order of priority, to the exclusion of all others.

Married individual

Particular Circumstances	*Division*
(1) Estate amounts to less than £125,000	All to spouse
(2) Estate exceeds £125,000 and there are children	Spouse is entitled to first £125,000 and a life interest in half the remainder. The balance is shared between the children
(3) Estate is worth less than £200,000 and there are no children	All to spouse
(4) Estate comes to more than £200,000, the couple have no children but parents are still alive	Spouse receives first £200,000 and half the remainder absolutely. The parents divide the rest
(5) As in (4) above, parents are dead, but there are brothers and sisters	As in (4) above but the balance is shared between the brothers and sisters instead of the parents
(6) The only survivor is the spouse	All to spouse

The spouse must survive the intestate individual by 28 days to become entitled under the intestacy rules.

In Scotland the intestacy rules have no application to estates of individuals who die domiciled there. Furthermore, a surviving spouse and/or children are entitled to fixed proportions of the moveable estate of the deceased individual. This rule applies whether the deceased died intestate or had made a will.

Legacies

Any Inheritance Tax due on a legacy you receive under a will will be accounted for by the executors of the estate before the legacy is paid over to you. You do not pay either Income Tax or Capital Gains Tax on a legacy. It does not need to be reported on your annual Tax Return.

17 TAX-SAVING HINTS

Saving tax is not always so straightforward as it sounds. To make a meaningful reduction in your annual tax bill will usually necessitate reorganizing your finances and investments. As a general rule opportunities to save tax should not be considered without due regard to other criteria.

First and foremost comes your own personal circumstances. Maybe you are a married man, and your wife has a low taxable income? You know that if you transfer some investments into her own name you can increase her income so she can benefit from her full personal allowance. If you are paying tax at 40% you should consider doing more to utilize your wife's bands of income taxable at 10% and at the lower rates on savings and dividend income. Alternatively, think about holding bank/building society accounts and other investments in your joint names. Either way you should be able to cut the family tax bill, perhaps significantly.

But remember that the investments given to your wife will then belong to her. Most couples will continue to enjoy the benefits from their saving in tax for many years to come. This is not so for everyone – some couples will split up. While no couple ever wants to contemplate that their marriage might break down, the prospect of this happening should, at the very least, be borne in mind in any tax-planning exercise involving a transfer of assets between spouses. The same rule applies if you are thinking about making gifts to your children. They have been known to squander money and subsequently fall out with their parents.

When it comes to investments, remember that you will sometimes need to be locked into an investment for a number of years to benefit from all the tax attractions that go with it. A typical example of this type of investment is a subscription for new shares in a Venture Capital Trust. Examine the merits of any investment from all angles. Sometimes it will be best to steer clear of investments that are inflexible. You could end up endangering your family's financial security. The same applies to those investments that carry a higher degree of risk.

Throughout life, from childhood to retirement, circumstances and priorities change. At every stage it is important to make well-informed decisions to ensure that you and your family are following the best strategies for achieving your goals. When it comes to tax you may need to adjust your finances to take account of future reductions or increases in the various taxes. You should also be ready to respond to any shift in taxation policy following a change in Government. Remember that when you focus on your estate plan it will be the law at some time in the future, when you die, which will determine the tax payable by your executors.

Self-Assessment

- Remember the key dates for Self-Assessment, particularly those for sending back your complete and signed Tax Return. These are 30 September and 31 January after the end of the tax year. You must send your return back by 30 September if you want the Inland Revenue to calculate your tax. The same date applies if you pay tax under PAYE, and want any underpayment of tax collected by an adjustment to your PAYE code number in the following year.

- Do not forget that the second send-back date of 31 January is critical. You must stick to it. Otherwise a fixed penalty will automatically be applied for the late return.

- The main dates of the forthcoming annual Self-Assessment calendar are summarized in Appendix 10 at the end of the book.

- Always answer 'yes' to question 19 on page 7 of your Tax Return. Any tax overpaid will then be refunded to you. Otherwise it is likely to be kept by the Inland Revenue for set-off against a future tax payment.

- If you have overpaid tax, carefully check the Inland Revenue's interest figures on the adjustment required to your Self-Assessment. There are times when the Inland Revenue's computer program does not produce the right calculation. As a result you may not have been given the right amount of tax-free interest on the repayment.

- If the amount of any of your sources of income is substantially different compared to the previous year, use the additional information box on page 8 to explain the reason for the change.

- Remember you can amend your Self-Assessment at any time up to the end of 12 months after the normal filing date.

- Keep proper records. You will find it easier to complete your Tax Return fully and accurately. Furthermore, if your tax office decides to enquire into your Tax Return the records you have kept will help you demonstrate that your Return is accurate and complete in all respects. Remember also to keep your records for the right length of time.

- Always pay your tax on time. If you are late in making payment then not only will you be charged interest but you also run the risk of incurring a surcharge.

Allowances and reliefs

- Every taxpayer, man or woman, single or married, is entitled to the personal allowance. Married couples should consider transferring their income-producing assets between them to maximize personal allowances and, where possible, the starting and/or savings and basic rate tax bands. Where this is inappropriate, joint ownership might be an alternative.

- Elderly married couples should not forget to consider whether the rules governing the transfer of the married couple's allowance between husband and wife can save them tax.

- Elderly couples need to pay even more care and attention to their respective incomes. They should make sure they do not lose out on the higher personal age and married couple's allowances for pensioners in the 65–74 and over 74 age brackets. They should keep an eye on the annual income limit above which allowances are restricted. It may pay them to shift some of their savings income into tax-free investments such as National Savings or ISAs. By doing so, they may avoid losing some of their age-related allowances.

- Remember that the income limit for the married couple's allowance is by reference to the husband's income. This always applies even if entitlement to this allowance arises because of the wife's age.

- Around each January/February look out for your new PAYE coding notice for the following tax year. Make sure you have been given the right allowances and that any deductions for unpaid tax or benefits-in-kind are correct. Get in touch with your tax office if anything is unclear.

- Don't delay sending in your claim for either the Child or Working Tax Credit. Claims can only be backdated for a maximum of three months.

Your job

- The company car continues to be an important part of the remuneration package for many employees. The system of taxing company cars aims to encourage the use of cleaner cars by linking the tax charge to the exhaust emission of the car. When you come to change your company car it will pay you to look into the CO_2 emission figure of the proposed replacement car. This could save you tax on your company car benefit.

- Do not overlook that there is no tax charge on parking spaces provided at, or near, your work place.

- The cost of petrol for private mileage paid for by your employer is a taxable benefit calculated on the CO_2 emission figure for your car. You will often be better off paying for your own petrol for non-business travel.

- Often it is better to own your own car and charge your employer for the cost of all your business mileage. But you must keep a proper and detailed mileage record.

- Perhaps your employer is paying you a mileage allowance for using your car, motorcycle or bicycle for business. You can claim tax relief on any difference between the amount you receive and the statutory rate.

- You are not taxable on any contributions made by your employer to your pension scheme or your own personal pension policy.

- Think about enquiring whether your employer operates one of the various share, profit sharing and share option schemes, all of which have different investment limits and tax relief. Perhaps membership of whatever scheme is on offer from your employer will be an attractive long-term investment with built-in tax advantages.

Value Added Tax

- If your business is not VAT registered, maintain a regular check on your turnover to make sure you are not exceeding the limit for registration.

- Sometimes it pays to apply for voluntary registration. You may be able to reclaim significant amounts of VAT on purchases for and expenses of your business. However, check on your customers to make sure they are VAT registered and will be able to reclaim the VAT charged on your invoices.

- If the annual turnover of your business is under £150,000, perhaps the Flat Rate Scheme is for you? It will save you time in dealing with the requirements of normal accounting for VAT.

- Look into the merits of the Annual or Cash Accounting Schemes if your annual turnover is less than £600,000.

Sole traders

- Do not forget to advise the Inland Revenue as soon as you become self-employed. There is a penalty of £100 if you do not tell them within 3 months of commencement.

- Then think about your accounting date. For the sake of convenience 31 March is an obvious choice as the date coincides with the end of the tax year. Sometimes, however, it is preferable to go with a date early on in the tax year, such as 30 April, as it allows more time to plan for the funding of the tax payable.

- Maintain proper books and records for your business. Make sure they are accurate and always up to date. Avoid using estimates.

- Where appropriate pay your wife a proper and fair salary for the secretarial or other assistance she gives you.

- Consider taking your wife into partnership where she helps you in your business and your annual profits are such that the top slice is taxable at the higher 40% rate.

- Where you incur mixed expenses – part business with the balance private – be careful over the apportionment calculation and only claim the business element as an expense for tax purposes.

- If you are thinking about buying plant and machinery or, for example, a new car, then it may be better to do so towards the end of your accounting year rather than early in the following year. You benefit from the capital allowances due on the expenditure at an earlier date.

- Explore all the options available for claiming tax relief due on a business loss. You may well find that one or other of the different alternative types of loss-relief claim produces a bigger tax repayment for you. In doing your calculations do not overlook the impact of the tax-free repayment supplement paid by the Inland Revenue.

- If your business is booming and is extremely profitable you should seriously think about transferring it to a limited company where you own the shares. This is one of those areas where you should seek advice from a tax specialist.

- Lastly, always look to the future and plan for your retirement whether you are contemplating a sale of your business or handing it down to the next generation.

Pensions

- Make pension savings play a significant role as part of your overall personal financial planning.

- Pension schemes offer, perhaps, the greatest scope for tax saving and planning which include:

  — Replacing your income when you retire

  — Tax relief on premiums at your top rate of tax

  — No UK tax payable by pension funds

  — Tax-free lump sum on retirement

  — Death benefits free of Inheritance Tax

- If you are in employment, look into joining your employer's Group or Stakeholder Pension Scheme. Consider topping up the pension benefits under the scheme by the payment of additional voluntary contributions. As an alternative you can pay up to £3,600 per annum into a Stakeholder Scheme provided your salary is not more than £30,000 a year.

- Keep a close eye on your annual earnings for pension purposes. Subject to the annual earnings limit the maximum contributions you can make each year into a personal pension plan are based on the higher of your salary or business profits for that tax year or in any of the five preceding tax years. This rule is of particular value to those in business with fluctuating profits.

- Maybe you are a non-earner, perhaps a person enjoying a career break or a non-earning spouse. You can now pay up to £3,600 gross p.a. into a pension plan. This allowance also extends to children where contributions can be paid for them by their parents or grandparents.

- If you have not been making the maximum contributions into your retirement annuity contract do not forget you are allowed to carry forward the unused relief for up to six years.

- Where you are still paying premiums into a retirement annuity taken out before the beginning of July 1988 it may be better to continue with this policy rather than start a personal pension plan. Do, however, bear in mind the higher annual contribution limits into a personal pension compared with a retirement annuity.

Tax-favoured investments

- Take a look at the investments available from National Savings and Investments where the return is free of both Income Tax and Capital Gains Tax.

- You can withdraw up to 5% per annum tax free each year from a non-qualifying life policy such as a single premium investment bond. This could be a good way to supplement your income.

- Make sure you are opening the right type of ISA. If you want to invest more than £3,000 in stocks and shares in any one tax year, you must open a maxi ISA. You can only subscribe to one maxi ISA each tax year. You cannot subscribe to a mini ISA and a maxi ISA in the same tax year. You can subscribe to up to three separate mini ISAs investing in each of the three different types of investments (stocks and shares, cash and life assurance) in the same tax year. You must not subscribe to more than one mini ISA investing in the same type of investment in each tax year.

- Continue with any existing TESSA. When it has matured you can transfer the capital in the account, but not the accumulated interest, into the cash component of an ISA without affecting the amount of new money that can be subscribed to an ISA.

- Although no new money can now be invested into your PEPs, you do not have to terminate any PEPs you hold. They can continue under the present rules with Income Tax and Capital Gains Tax benefits similar to those that you have enjoyed in the past.

- Venture Capital Trusts are tax-efficient vehicles aimed at encouraging investment in unquoted companies in the UK. Bear in mind, therefore, that an investment in a Venture Capital Trust carries a higher degree of risk. The tax benefits for a 'qualifying subscriber' are:

  — 20% Income Tax relief on the amount invested up to £100,000

  — Deferral of Capital Gains Tax on gains reinvested

  — Tax-free income and capital gains

- Investments under the Enterprise Investment Scheme are also high risk with generous tax benefits.

Capital Gains

- Wherever possible try to utilize fully your annual Capital Gains Tax exemption limit. Any part of the limit not used cannot be carried forward to future years.

- Husband and wife each have their own annual exemption limit. They should consider transferring assets between them, either to use up both exemption limits or to realize gains taxed at a lower rate on one spouse compared to the other.

- Do not forget that the excess of your chargeable gains over and above the exemption limit is charged at the tax rates found by adding the excess to your taxable income. By realizing losses you may be able to substantially reduce your Capital Gains Tax liability – particularly if you are a 40% taxpayer.

- Perhaps you have sold some assets and face a substantial Capital Gains Tax bill on the profits realized? Then why not consider investing under the Enterprise Investment Scheme or in Venture Capital Trust Shares? Only the gain, not the sale proceeds, needs to be reinvested.

- Where it is to your advantage, do not overlook making an election for the gains and losses on disposals of assets which you owned on 31 March 1982 to be calculated solely by reference to their market value at that date. The time limit for making the election is two years after the end of the tax year in which the first disposal of an asset you owned on 31 March 1982 takes place.

- When you fill in your Tax Return have regard to the types of business asset that attract the much more generous rate of taper relief in working out chargeable gains on disposals of such assets.

Your home

- If you have two homes, you are allowed to make an election stipulating which of your homes you want to be regarded as your principal private residence for Capital Gains Tax purposes where the profit on sale is free of tax. Remember that the election must be made within two years from the date when two or more properties are eligible and can subsequently be varied.

- The last three years of ownership of a property, which at some point in time has been your only or main residence, are always treated as though they were occupied as the main residence.

- Where a property that has been let has also been lived in as a main residence there is an additional relief from the taxable gain relating to the let period up to a maximum £40,000.

- Husband and wife should consider owning a second home jointly. This should help reduce the Capital Gains Tax payable on a future sale as they both may be able to take advantage of their own annual exemption limits in working out the tax payable on a profit on a sale.

- If your job takes you away from home for up to four years, your period away from home will still count as if you were in occupation of your main residence. The same applies for an unlimited period during which you work full time overseas.

- It is not uncommon for unmarried couples to own a home each. They may each be able to nominate a main residence for capital gains purposes.

Miscellaneous

- Now that you can no longer get tax relief on mortgage interest to buy your own home, it might be worthwhile to use any spare cash on deposit with a bank or building society to repay some or all of your mortgage.

- Make your charitable donations under the Gift Aid Scheme. Charities can then further benefit by claiming repayment from the Inland Revenue of the tax you deduct and retain at the basic rate. If you are liable to tax at the top rate of 40% you will also profit as you can deduct such payments in working out your annual higher-rate tax liability.

- Non-taxpayers should get the special form so they can receive their bank and building society interest gross, that is with no deduction for tax. Non-taxpayers are most likely to be pensioners, children or dependent married women.

- You would be well advised to look into taking out a loan to assist in financing the purchase of an investment property which you then intend to let out. This way you will be able to claim the annual interest on the borrowing as a deduction against the net rents received from the property.

- If you are letting furnished accommodation in your home, consider whether you can benefit from Rent-a-Room relief. Gross annual rents below £4,250 are tax free.

- Non-residents with property in the United Kingdom which is let should consider putting their homes into joint ownership. It could then be possible for both spouses to claim their personal allowances in working out the tax payable on their respective shares of the rental income.

- Foreign nationals living in the UK should make the most of their non-UK domicile status for tax purposes. Such individuals are not subject to UK taxation on either overseas investment income or capital gains unless the investment income or capital gains are remitted to, or enjoyed in, the UK.

- Grandparents, or other relatives with the means, can fund tax efficiently for school fees and other costs of educating and maintaining children. This is best done via a Trust. The income the

Trustees pay out counts as the children's income for tax purposes. They should be able to reclaim all or part of the tax suffered by the Trustees by off-setting it against their personal allowance.

Inheritance Tax

- Remember that gifts and transfers between husbands and wives are exempt from Inheritance Tax.

- Whenever you can afford to do so, make use of the various exemptions detailed in Chapter 16.

- The *'normal expenditure out of income'* exemption is ideal for paying premiums on life policies written in Trust for the next generations. The policy proceeds will pass to them free of tax. This is an effective method of dealing with an Inheritance Tax liability on death which cannot be avoided.

- While both gifts and legacies to charities are exempt for Inheritance Tax purposes, a lifetime gift of cash or shares to a charity can have attractive Income Tax and Capital Gains Tax benefits for the donor.

- Gifts outside the exemptions should be made as early as possible to increase your chances of surviving the seven-year period. Make immediately chargeable gifts – for example to Discretionary Settlements – before potentially exempt transfers.

- Give assets that do not qualify for relief before those that do.

- Gift assets with low values so that the appreciation accrues to the recipient and outside of your estate.

- Make a will. Otherwise your estate will devolve under the intestacy laws and not in a way that you want. Keep your will up to date.

- Consider restricting chargeable legacies for the next generations to the nil rate band, leaving the rest of your estate to your spouse. He or she can then make gifts and hopefully survive a further seven years.

- Do not waste your nil rate band. Even if you want to leave everything to your spouse, ask about Discretionary Wills. The potential saving in tax for the next generations is significant.

- Where possible look into rearranging your affairs to take advantage of the business or agricultural property reliefs.

- In the two years after death, consider the use of a Deed of Variation in order to utilize any available exemptions that would otherwise be lost.

18 APPENDICES

1 Inland Revenue Explanatory Booklets

No.	Title
IR 1	Extra Statutory Concessions
IR 3	Personal Pension Schemes
IR 14/15	Construction Industry Scheme
IR 20	Residents and Non-Residents – Liability to Tax in the United Kingdom
IR 33	Income Tax and School Leavers
IR 34	Pay As You Earn
IR 37	Appeals against Tax
IR 40	Conditions for getting a Sub-Contractor's Tax Certificate
IR 41	Income Tax and Jobseekers
IR 45	What to do about Tax when Someone Dies
IR 56	Employed or Self-Employed? A Guide for Tax and National Insurance
IR 59	Collection of Student Loans
IR 60	Students and the Inland Revenue
IR 64	Giving to Charity by Businesses
IR 65	Giving to Charity by Individuals
IR 68	Accrued Income Scheme: Taxing Securities on Transfer
IR 72	Investigations: The Examination of Business Accounts
IR 73	Inland Revenue Investigations: How Settlements are Negotiated
IR 78	Looking to the future: Tax Reliefs to help you save for retirement
IR 87	Letting and your Home
IR 95	Approved Profit-Sharing Schemes – An Outline for Employees
IR 97	Approved SAYE Share Option Schemes – An Outline for Employees Schemes
IR 101	Approved Company Share Option Plans – An Outline for Employees
IR 110	A Guide for People with Savings
IR 115	Income Tax, National Insurance Contributions and Childcare
IR 116	Guide for Sub-Contractors with Tax Certificates
IR 117	Guide for Sub-Contractors with Registration Cards
IR 119	Tax Relief for Vocational Training

IR 121	Income Tax and Pensioners
IR 122	Volunteer Drivers
IR 124	Using Your Own Vehicle for Work
IR 125	Using Your Own Car or Motorbike for Work
IR 131	Inland Revenue Statements of Practice
IR 134	Income Tax and Relocation Packages
IR 136	Income Tax and Company Vans
IR 137	The Enterprise Investment Scheme
IR 138	Living or Retiring Abroad? A guide to UK tax on your UK income and pension
IR 139	Income from Abroad? A guide to UK tax on overseas income
IR 140	Non-Resident Landlords, their Agents and Tenants
IR 141	Open Government
IR 143	Income Tax and Redundancy
IR 144	Income Tax and Incapacity Benefit
IR 145	Low Interest Loans Provided by Employers
IR 150	Taxation of Rents – A Guide to Property Income
IR 152	Trusts: An Introduction
IR 153	Tax Exemption for Sickness or Unemployment Insurance Payments
IR 155	PAYE Settlement Agreements
IR 160	Inland Revenue Enquiries under Self-Assessment
IR 167	Charter for Inland Revenue Taxpayers
IR 169	Venture Capital Trusts (VCTs) – A Brief Guide
IR 170	Blind Person's Allowance
IR 171	Income Tax: A Guide for People With Children
IR 172	Income Tax and Company Cars
IR 176	Tax, National Insurance Contributions and Green Travel
IR 177	Share Incentive Plans and Your Entitlement to Benefits
IR 178	Giving Shares and Securities to Charity
SA/BK3	Self-Assessment – A Guide to Keeping Records for the Self-Employed
SA/BK4	Self-Assessment – A General Guide to Keeping Records
SA/BK6	Self-Assessment – Penalties for Late Tax Returns
SA/BK7	Self-Assessment – Surcharges for Late Payment of Tax
SA/BK8	Self-Assessment – Your Guide
480	Expenses and Benefits: A Tax Guide
CGT 1	Capital Gains Tax: A Quick Guide
IHT 2	Inheritance Tax on Lifetime Gifts
IHT 3	Inheritance Tax: An Introduction
IHT 14	Inheritance Tax: The Personal Representative's Responsibilities
COP 11	Enquiries into Tax Returns by Local Tax Offices
CTC/BK1	Help With the Cost of Childcare
WTC 1	Child Tax Credit and Working Tax Credit – A Guide

2 Flat-Rate Allowances for Special Clothing and the Upkeep of Tools – 2003/04

(1)	*Fixed rate for all occupations*	£
	Agricultural	70
	Forestry	70
	Quarrying	70
	Brass and copper	100
	Precious metals	70
	Textile prints	60
	Food	40
	Glass	60
	Railways (non-crafts people)	70
	Uniformed prison officers	55
	Uniformed bank employees	40
	Uniformed police officers up to and including chief inspector	55
	Uniformed fire fighters and fire officers	60

(2)	*Variable rate depending on category of occupation*	£
	Seamen	130/135
	Iron mining	75/100
	Iron and steel	45/60/120
	Aluminium	45/60/100/130
	Engineering	45/60/100/120
	Shipyards	45/60/75/115
	Vehicles	40/60/105
	Particular engineering	45/60/100/120
	Constructional engineering	45/60/75/115
	Electrical and electricity supply	25/90
	Textiles	60/85
	Clothing	30/45
	Leather	40/55
	Printing	30/70/105
	Building materials	40/55/85
	Wood and furniture	45/75/90/115
	Building	40/55/85/105
	Heating	70/90/100
	Public service	40/55
	Healthcare	45/60/70/110

Note   The allowances are only available to manual workers who have to bear the cost of upkeep of tools and special clothing. Other employees, such as office staff, cannot claim them.

3 VAT Notices and Leaflets

No.	Title
48	Extra Statutory Concessions
700	The VAT Guide
700/1	Should I be Registered for VAT?
700/11	Cancelling your Registration
700/12	Filling in your VAT Return
700/15	The Ins and Outs of VAT
700/21	Keeping Records and Accounts
700/41	Late Registration: Penalty
700/42	Misdeclaration Penalties
700/43	Default Interest
700/45	How to Correct VAT Errors and make Adjustments or Claims
700/50	Default Surcharge
727	Retail Schemes
731	Cash Accounting
732	Annual Accounting
733	Flat Rate Scheme for Small Businesses
930	What if I don't pay?
989	Visits by Customs and Excise Officers
999	Catalogue of Publications
1000	Complaints and Putting Things Right

4 Rates of National Insurance Contributions for 2003/04

CLASS 1 Contributions for Employees

Contributions levied on all weekly earnings above £89.00 but which do not exceed £595.00:

Standard Rate: 11%

Contracted Out: 9.4%

Reduced Rate for Married Women and Widows with a Valid Election Certificate: 4.85%

Contributions levied on all weekly earnings in excess of £595.00: 1%

Rate for Men over 65 and Women over 60: Nil

Earnings Threshold	Weekly	£89.00
	Monthly:	£385.00
	Annual:	£4,615.00
Upper Earnings Limit	Weekly:	£595.00
	Monthly:	£2,576.00
	Annual:	£30,940.00

CLASS 2 Contributions for the Self-Employed

Weekly flat rate: £2.00

Small earnings exception: £4,095.00

CLASS 3 Voluntary Contributions

Weekly rate: £6.95

CLASS 4 Contributions for the Self-Employed

On profits between £4,615 and £30,940: 8%

On profits in excess of £30,940: 1%

5 National Insurance Explanatory Leaflets

No.	Title
CA01	National Insurance Contributions for Employees
CA02	National Insurance Contributions for Self-Employed People with Small Earnings
CA04	National Insurance Contributions: Class 2 and Class 3 Direct Debit – The Easier Way to Pay
CA07	National Insurance Contributions – Unpaid and Late-Paid Contributions
CA08	National Insurance Contributions – Voluntary Contributions
CA09	National Insurance Contributions for Widows or Widowers
CA10	National Insurance Contributions for Divorcees
CA12	Training for Further Employment and Your NI Record
CA13	National Insurance Contributions for Married Women with Reduced Elections
CA 17	Employees' Guide to Minimum Contributions
CWL 2	National Insurance Contributions for Self-Employed People: Class 2 and Class 4

6 Social Security Benefits

Taxable
Incapacity Benefit after the first 28 weeks (1)
Industrial Death Benefit Pensions
Jobseeker's Allowance
Retirement Pension (1)
Carer's Allowance
Statutory Adoption Pay
Statutory Maternity and Paternity Pay
Statutory Sick Pay
Widowed Parent's Allowance (1)
Bereavement Allowance

Non-taxable
Incapacity Benefit for the first 28 weeks
Income Support
Adoption Pay
Maternity Allowance
Child Benefit
Child Tax Credit
Child's Special Allowance
Guardian's Allowance
One-Parent Benefit
Christmas Bonus for Pensioners
Industrial Injury Benefits
War Disablement Benefits
Disability Living Allowance
Bereavement Payment
Earnings Top-Up
Housing Benefit
Jobfinder's Grant
War Widow's, Widower's or Dependant's Pension
Social Fund Payments
Attendance Allowance
Council Tax Benefit
Redundancy Payment
Vaccine Damage (Lump Sum)
Television Licence Payment
Cold Weather and Winter Fuel Payments
Working Tax Credit

Note   (1) Child dependency additions to these benefits are not taxable.

7 Rates of Main Social Security Benefits for 2003/04

Weekly Rate from 07.04.2003 Onwards
£

Taxable

Retirement pensions

Single person	77.45
Married couple's: both contributors – each	77.45
wife not contributor – addition	46.35
Age addition (over 80) – each	0.25

Bereavement benefits

Bereavement allowance/widow's pension – maximum	77.45
Widowed parent's allowance	77.45

Jobseeker's allowance

Under age 18	32.90
Age 18 to 24	43.25
Age 25 or over	54.65

Incapacity benefit

Long-term	72.15
Increase for age: higher rate	15.15
lower rate	7.60
Short-term (under pension age): lower rate	54.40
higher rate	64.35
(over pension age): lower rate	69.20
higher rate	72.15

Statutory sick pay

Standard rate (weekly earnings threshold £77)	64.35

Statutory maternity, paternity and adoption pay

Rate (weekly earnings threshold £77)	100.00

Non-taxable

Maternity allowance

Standard rate	100.00

Child benefit

Only or eldest child (couple)	16.05
Each other child	10.75
Only or eldest child (lone parent)	17.55

Attendance allowance

Higher rate	57.20
Lower rate	38.30

8   Scope of Liability to Income Tax of Earnings

		Duties of employment performed wholly or partly in the UK		Duties of employment performed wholly outside the UK
		In the UK	Outside the UK	
Foreign emoluments[1]	Employee resident and ordinarily resident in the UK	Liable	Liable	Liable if received in the UK
	Resident but not ordinarily resident	Liable	Liable if received in the UK	Liable if received in the UK
	Not resident	Liable	Not liable	Not liable
Other earnings	Resident and ordinarily resident	Liable	Liable	Liable
	Resident but not ordinarily resident	Liable	Liable if received in the UK	Liable if received in the UK
	Not resident	Liable	Not liable	Not liable

Note   (1) 'Foreign emoluments' is the term to mean the earnings of someone who is not domiciled in the UK and whose employer is not resident in, and is resident outside, the UK.

9 Capital Gains Tax – The Indexation Allowance: April 1998

Starting Months and Years for Indexation

	1982	1983	1984	1985	1986	1987
January	–	0.968	0.872	0.783	0.689	0.626
February	–	0.960	0.865	0.769	0.683	0.620
March	1.047	0.956	0.859	0.752	0.681	0.616
April	1.006	0.929	0.834	0.716	0.665	0.597
May	0.992	0.921	0.828	0.708	0.662	0.596
June	0.987	0.917	0.823	0.704	0.663	0.596
July	0.986	0.906	0.825	0.707	0.667	0.597
August	0.985	0.898	0.808	0.703	0.662	0.593
September	0.987	0.889	0.804	0.704	0.654	0.588
October	0.977	0.883	0.793	0.701	0.652	0.580
November	0.967	0.876	0.788	0.695	0.638	0.573
December	0.971	0.871	0.789	0.693	0.632	0.574

	1988	1989	1990	1991	1992	1993
January	0.574	0.465	0.361	0.249	0.199	0.179
February	0.568	0.454	0.353	0.242	0.193	0.171
March	0.562	0.448	0.339	0.237	0.189	0.167
April	0.537	0.423	0.300	0.222	0.171	0.156
May	0.531	0.414	0.288	0.218	0.167	0.152
June	0.525	0.409	0.283	0.213	0.167	0.153
July	0.524	0.408	0.282	0.215	0.171	0.156
August	0.507	0.404	0.269	0.213	0.171	0.151
September	0.500	0.395	0.258	0.208	0.166	0.146
October	0.485	0.384	0.248	0.204	0.162	0.147
November	0.478	0.372	0.251	0.199	0.164	0.148
December	0.474	0.369	0.252	0.198	0.168	0.146

	1994	1995	1996	1997	1998
January	0.151	0.114	0.083	0.053	0.019
February	0.144	0.107	0.078	0.049	0.014
March	0.141	0.102	0.073	0.046	0.011
April	0.128	0.091	0.066	0.040	–
May	0.124	0.087	0.063	0.036	–
June	0.124	0.085	0.063	0.032	–
July	0.129	0.091	0.067	0.032	–
August	0.124	0.085	0.062	0.026	–
September	0.121	0.080	0.057	0.021	–
October	0.120	0.085	0.057	0.019	–
November	0.119	0.085	0.057	0.019	–
December	0.114	0.079	0.053	0.016	–

10 Main Dates of the Self-Assessment Calendar 6 April 2004 – 5 April 2005

Date	What happens	Who is affected
6 April 2004	2003/04 Tax Returns sent out by the Inland Revenue.	Taxpayers who need to fill in an annual Tax Return.
31 July 2004	Second payment on account due for 2003/04.	Those taxpayers who make regular half-yearly payments on account.
	Second £100 penalty levied for failing to submit a 2002/03 Tax Return.	Taxpayers who have not yet completed and sent back their 2002/03 Tax Returns.
	Further automatic 5% surcharge on tax still outstanding for 2002/03.	Late payers of tax still due for 2002/03.
30 September 2004	First filing deadline for completing and returning 2003/04 Tax Returns.	Taxpayers who want the Inland Revenue to: • calculate their tax for 2003/04 • collect tax owing for 2003/04 of less than £2,000 through their code number in 2005/06.
31 January 2005	Filing deadline for 2003/04 Tax Returns.	Taxpayers sent a 2003/04 Tax Return.
	Payment date for the balance of tax due for 2003/04 and the first payment on account for 2004/05.	Taxpayers who need to settle either of these liabilities.
1 February 2005	First penalty of £100 charged for the late filing of a 2003/04 Tax Return.	Taxpayers who were sent a 2003/04 Tax Return.
28 February 2005	First automatic 5% surcharge imposed for failing to pay tax due for 2003/04.	Late payers of tax for 2003/04.

19 2004 BUDGET MEASURES

2004/2005 Personal Allowances

	£
Personal	
aged under 65	4,745
aged 65–74	6,830
aged 75 and over	6,950
Married Couples	
born before 6 April 1935 and aged less than 75	*5,725
aged 75 and over	*5,795
minimum amount	*2,210
Income limit for age-related allowances	18,900
Relief for blind person (each)	1,560

* Indicates allowances where tax relief is restricted to 10%.

Tax Rates and Bands for 2004/05

Band of Taxable Income	Rate of Tax	Tax on Band	Cumulative Tax
£	%	£	£
0–2,020	10	202.00	202.00
2,021–31,400	22	6,436.60	6,665.60
over 31,400	40		

Rates of National Insurance Contributions for 2004/05

CLASS 1 Contributions for Employees

Contributions levied on all weekly earnings above £91 but which do not exceed £610:

Standard Rate: 11%

Contracted Out: 9.4%

Reduced Rate for Married Women and Widows with a Valid Election Certificate: 4.85%

Contributions levied on weekly earnings in excess of £610: 1%

Rate for Men over 65 and Women over 60: Nil

Earnings Threshold	Weekly	£91
	Monthly	£395
	Annual	£4,745
Upper Earnings Limit	Weekly	£610
	Monthly	£2,644
	Annual	£31,720

CLASS 2 Contributions for the Self-Employed

Weekly flat rate: £2.05

Small Earnings Exception: £4,215

CLASS 3 Voluntary Contributions

Weekly rate: £7.15

CLASS 4 Contributions for the Self-Employed

On profits between £4,745 and £31,720: 8%

On profits in excess of £31,720: 1%

Tax Credits

The child element of Child Tax Credit is increased by £180 to £1,625 per annum for each child from April 2004, an increase of about £3.50 a week.

Furthermore, the disabled child elements of Child Tax Credit and the various elements of the Working Tax Credit are increased for 2004/05 in line with inflation.

Pension Scheme Earnings Limit

Pension contributions for members of occupational pension schemes established on or after 14 March 1989, and for members joining schemes established before that date on or after 1 June 1989, are restricted to those based on a maximum annual earnings limit. This earnings cap is increased from £99,000 to £102,000 from 6 April 2004. It also applies to all personal pension schemes.

Company car fuel

If an employee receives free fuel for a company car, there is an additional taxable benefit. This is calculated by applying the company car tax percentage to a set figure. For 2004/05 this figure will be frozen at £14,400.

Employer provided vans

New rules are being introduced to calculate the amount of taxable benefit arising where an employee is provided with a van by his or her employer, and the van is made available for private use. At present, the benefit on a van available for private use is £500, or £350 if the van is more than four years old at the end of the tax year. This charge includes any private fuel provided.

From 6 April 2005, no charge will apply to employees who have to take their van home and are not allowed any other private use. Those employees with unrestricted private use will continue to incur the £500 or £350 scale charge, depending on the age of the van.

In a further measure which will impact on 6 April 2007, the discount for older vans will no longer apply and the scale charge will increase to £3,000 for employees with unrestricted private use. If fuel is also provided for private use an additional charge of £500 will be levied.

Employer Supported Childcare

From 6 April 2005 employees will be able to receive up to £50 a week free of both income tax and National Insurance where their employers:

- contract with an approved child carer; or

- provide child care vouchers for the purpose of paying an approved child carer.

Where an employer operates such a scheme it must be made available to all employees.

Venture Capital Trusts (VCTs)

In order to give a temporary stimulus to investment in VCTs the rate of income tax relief for investments in qualifying VCT shares is increased from 20% to 40% in relation to shares issued during the 2004/05 and 2005/06 tax years.

Furthermore, the annual investment limit increases from £100,000 to £200,000 for shares acquired on or after 6 April 2004.

Enterprise Investment Scheme (EIS)

To further encourage individuals to invest through the EIS the annual investment limit increases from £150,000 to £200,000 in respect of shares acquired on or after 6 April 2004.

Jointly owned shares in close companies – married couples

The Chancellor has announced that income arising from jointly owned shares in close companies will no longer automatically be divided equally between husband and wife. With effect from 6 April 2004, such income (usually in the form of dividend distributions) will now be taxed according to the actual proportions of ownership and entitlement to income.

Simplification of the Taxation of Pensions

From 6 April 2006, one year later than originally anticipated, the 8 existing tax regimes for pensions will be replaced by a single set of rules for all tax privileged pension plans.

Under current law there are different rules governing contributions to, and benefits secured by, plans ranging from occupational schemes through to personal pensions.

Simplification will remove all these controls. In their place will be just one set of rules governing all schemes.

The key elements of the new system will be:

- A single lifetime allowance, which will be reviewed quinquennially, on the amount of an individual's pension savings that can benefit from tax relief. This allowance will be set at £1.5 million on introduction in April 2006 rising to £1.6 million in 2007, £1.65 million in 2008, £1.75 million in 2009 and £1.8 million in 2010.

- An annual contributions allowance, initially set at £215,000. Although it will be reviewed quinquennially it will increase steadily each year such that by 2010 it will be at £255,000 for payments to defined contribution schemes or increases in accrued benefits in defined benefit schemes.

- Contributions will no longer be limited to a percentage of capped earnings. Subject to the annual allowance, individuals will be able to make unlimited contributions up to the higher of 100% of relevant earnings and £3,600 per annum.

- On retirement up to 25% of the value of the fund can be taken as a tax-free cash sum. However, under simplification, the maximum permissible tax-free lump sum cannot exceed 25% of the lifetime allowance.

- The minimum pension age will rise from 50 to 55 by 2010.

- It will continue to be a requirement that pensions are taken by age 75.

- It will no longer be necessary for a member to leave employment in order to access pension under an employers Occupational Pension Scheme. Providing it is allowed under the Scheme rules, members of Occupational Pension Schemes will be allowed to continue working for the same employer while, at the same time, drawing Retirement Benefits.

- Death benefits from a scheme can be in the form of either a lump sum, a pension to one or more dependents or a combination of lump sum and pension.

- A recovery charge will be payable where an individual has built up benefits in excess of the lifetime allowance at the date of retirement. This charge will be levied at the rate of 25% on the value of funds in excess of the lifetime allowance. But it will be possible for an individual to receive payment as a lump sum of the value of funds in excess of the lifetime allowance, in which case this charge increases to 55%.

- Transitional arrangements will protect pension rights built up before 6 April 2006, including two options for transitional protection from the lifetime allowance charge.

- Contributions paid to a registered Pension Scheme by an employer will still be deductible in computing profits chargeable to UK tax. The current practice of spreading tax relief on large contributions over 2–4 years will continue.

Capital Allowances

The rate of first-year allowances for small businesses spending on plant and machinery will be increased from 40% to 50% for one year from 1 April 2004. For medium-sized enterprises the rate remains unchanged at 40%.

Value Added Tax

The Value Added Tax registration threshold is increased with effect from 1 April 2004 from annual taxable turnover of £56,000 to £58,000. The cancellation of registration limit goes up from £54,000 to £56,000.

From the start of their next accounting period after 1 May 2004 businesses must use the new scale charges for motor fuel as shown in the following table:

| | Diesel | | Other | |
Car Engine Size – cc	Scale Charge £	VAT £	Scale Charge £	VAT £
1400 or less	216.00	32.17	232.00	34.55
1401 to 2000	216.00	32.17	293.00	43.63
Over 2000	273.00	40.65	432.00	64.34

From 1 April 2004 businesses with an annual taxable turnover of between £600,000 and £660,000 will, for the first time, be able to join the VAT Cash and Annual Accounting Schemes. Businesses already using these schemes will be able to continue to do so until their annual taxable turnover reaches £825,000.

Capital Gains Tax

The Capital Gains Tax annual exemption limit is increased to £8,100

Venture Capital Trust shares issued on or after 6 April 2004 will not qualify for Capital Gains Tax deferral relief. The relief does, however, remain available in respect of gains arising in the 2004/05 tax year where the Venture Capital Trust shares in question were issued before 6 April 2004 but within the period of 12 months ending on the date the gain arose.

Inheritance Tax

From 6 April 2004 the nil rate band increases from £255,000 to £263,000.

In order to bring the Inheritance Tax penalty rules more into line with those for Income and Capital Gains Taxes the following penalties are proposed:

- A penalty of £100 will be charged for the late delivery of an Inheritance Tax account.

- A penalty of up to £3,000 will be charged for failure to submit an Inheritance Tax account.

- Current penalties chargeable as a result of negligent or fraudulent returns will not be charged where no additional Inheritance Tax arises.

Those individuals who have made gifts of assets during their lifetime in order to alleviate the eventual Inheritance Tax burden on their estates will now face an annual income tax charge if they still enjoy the use of the asset in question. This measure takes effect from 6 April 2005. It will also cover cases where one asset is replaced by another. The amount of the benefit will be dependent on the value of the asset, property for example will be based on the market rent and for other assets such as works of art or antiques, a capital value will be charged at the Inland Revenue's 'official rate' of interest. This broadly follows the current model of benefit-in-kind charges on employees.

The benefit will be reduced where:

- Rent is paid for the use of the asset.

- The donor has expressly reserved a right to occupation of the property when making the gift.

Any calculated cash value of below £2,500 will be disregarded (i.e. asset values not exceeding £50,000).

The charge will *not* apply where:

- The asset was gifted before 18 March 1986.

- The asset gifted is currently owned by the taxpayer's spouse.

- The asset would form part of the taxpayer's estate for Inheritance Tax purposes under the existing 'gift with reservation' rules.

- The asset in question was originally sold at an arms' length price.

- The asset in question was inherited and transferred as part of a Deed of Variation of the will.

- Any enjoyment of the asset is no more than incidental.

Importantly, former owners will not be regarded as enjoying a taxable benefit if they retain an interest, which is consistent with their ongoing enjoyment of the property. For example, no charge will arise where an elderly parent formerly owning the whole of their home passes a half share to a child who lives with them.

In recognition of the fact that it may not be desirable to dismantle existing tax-driven schemes a special transitional treatment is proposed. Taxpayers will be able to elect, by 31 January 2007, to treat the asset in question as part of their taxable estate for Inheritance Tax. If this election is made no income tax charge will arise.

Exactly how this will be policed is as yet unclear but it certainly presents a minefield for those who have previously used a perfectly adequate form of tax planning to help preserve their estate for the next generation.

Non-Compliance

The Government is determined to crack down on those who fail to comply with their legal obligations such as paying their tax or filing their Tax Return on time. The Inland Revenue have been provided with additional funding to target:

- non-payment of tax and National Insurance;

- failure to file a Tax Return on time;

- undeclared income or profits offshore;

- avoidance of Corporation Tax and of National Insurance on employment income.

The package of measures will be implemented very shortly and introduced over the forthcoming months.

Simplified Self-Assessment Tax Return

This is a welcome change for those whose Self-Assessment Tax Returns are simple, for example, have straightforward investment income and is aimed at:

- employees (other than directors);

- small businesses (a self-employed individual with a turnover of less than £15,000);

- pensioners who receive the state pension, an occupational pension or a retirement annuity.

The simplified Tax Return will be just four pages and the idea is that the form be filed by 30 September so that the Inland Revenue can calculate the tax position and what to pay by the following January. The short form will be issued automatically based on the information reported on the Tax Return for the previous year but there will still be a responsibility if circumstances change such that the short form is not appropriate.

It is expected that this will impact from April 2004 for some 400,000 individuals and then nationally from April 2005 when it is expected that around 500,000 will be affected.